THE NETHERLANDS INDIES
AND JAPAN

Their Relations 1940-1941

THE NETHERLANDS INDIES AND JAPAN

Their Relations 1940-1941

by

Dr. H. J. VAN MOOK

London
GEORGE ALLEN & UNWIN LTD

FIRST PUBLISHED IN 1944

E000088401

940.5349301

M 17316

BOOK
PRODUCTION
WAR ECONOMY
STANDARD

*This Book is Produced in Complete
Conformity with the Authorised
Economy Standards*

PRINTED IN GREAT BRITAIN AT
THE UNIVERSITY PRESS
ABERDEEN

PREFACE

" Send danger from the north unto the south,
So honour cross it from the east to west."

HISTORY should be written a long time after it is made, with full access to sources, and dispassionate criticism. On the other hand, it may be useful to relate events that happened, in part at least, beyond the public ken, as soon as circumstances permit and while their recollection is still vivid in the memory of the participants. It can prevent the growth of legends which usually crop up around semi-secret proceedings of political importance and confuse our judgment in after years. A more precise knowledge of past occurrences can aid us in understanding the present and even in shaping our course towards the future.

The story told in this little book is such a chronicle of facts concerning the relations between the Netherlands in Asia and Japan during the last two years before the outbreak of war in the Pacific. Its scope is limited to political and economic affairs of which the author has a first-hand knowledge; comments and background sketching have been restricted to what seemed indispensable. There have been other and more romantic descriptions, but most of the material adduced here has been inaccessible until now; it is published with the kind co-operation of the Netherland Minister of Foreign Affairs, Dr. van Kleffens. It will serve to bring several things into a truer focus.

In the first place these relations have been far too often interpreted as a matter of individual action and skill. People are apt to identify currents of public opinion with the names of those who are the more or less faithful exponents thereof;

their sense of the dramatic makes them concentrate their attention on the actors who were picked out by the limelight of publicity, whereas they overlook the part played by the producers and the audience. In a country where public men are not surrounded by black guards or detectives, where the press is uncensored, and where discussion of national and international affairs is free and searching—and all this applied to the Netherlands Indies as well as to the Netherlands—international policy cannot be conducted like some sort of mystery by a few adepts ; it must be rooted in public sentiment and acceptable to public intelligence. With the Netherlands occupied by Nazi terror, the Government found their main strength in a practically unanimous support by the citizenry of all races in the Indies. Not only did the better educated layers of the population—including many hundred thousands of Indonesians and Indo-Chinese—approve ; even the masses had become aware of the Japanese danger through four years of spreading reports and rumours from China.

During the negotiations in Batavia the Government and the Netherland delegation were assisted by a large advisory committee of Netherland and Indonesian experts. They found no difficulty in reaching generally agreed conclusions which could be based on well-established and commonly accepted principles of economic policy. These principles are to be found in the memoranda of 3rd February and 6th June 1941.[1] On this sound and solid foundation the team-work of the delegation was excellent and needed little special management. The Press, including the vernacular papers and those of the nationalist opposition, was wholly and explicitly behind the Government in this respect. On the 25th of June the representative assembly, the Volksraad, consisting of 31 Indonesian, 5 Chinese and Arab, and 25 Netherland members,[2] gave their final appreciation of the

---

[1] See pp. 72 and 88.

[2] A majority of the last group consisting of people born and bred in the Indies.

Netherland-Japanese discussions in their committee report on the budget for 1942.[1] Remarking on the fact that the people in the Indies had shown great restraint and complete confidence in the policy of the Government throughout, it praised, without a dissenting voice, the firm and reasonable attitude maintained during those discussions. It said : " Although the negotiations did not lead to a mutually satisfactory conclusion, the preservation of the integrity of the Indies, notwithstanding strong pressure from the other side, and, at the same time, the continuation of normal relations with Japan, constitute an exceptionally favourable result, which is further enhanced by the gain of prestige for the Netherlands Indies within and without."

The same report unanimously paid homage to Her Majesty the Queen, voicing the general admiration and gratitude for Her inspiring leadership. These were no empty words. The fact that the Queen and Her Government had retained their liberty of action was a strong, if not a decisive element in the position of the Indies and their relations with Japan. Had it been otherwise, although the Indies would certainly not have given way like Indo-China, the temptation to interfere, both on the Allied and the enemy side, would have been much greater. The Netherland Government in London needed no outside assistance ; they could rely as firmly on public opinion in the Netherlands Indies as on the unbroken resistance in the Netherlands. They were ably seconded by a great Governor-General. The high character and the penetrating intelligence of Jhr. Tjarda van Starkenborgh were a full guarantee against vacillating or erratic decisions, and his wide diplomatic experience gave invaluable guidance to the tactical work of the Netherland delegation. He remained resolute and unshakable to the end.

[1] This report contains a survey of political and economic conditions and desires and a general discussion of the budget ; it answers the opening speech of the Governor-General and the memorandum, which accompanies the budget. The budget is presented annually at the opening of the session.

A rather widespread misconception resulted from one of the more consistent lies of the Japanese propaganda machine. The Netherland attitude was continuously depicted in the Nippon Press as one of endless procrastination and duplicity ; newspaper stories elsewhere began to credit us with an almost Machiavellian craftiness. The reader will see for himself that nothing was less true. We certainly wanted to gain time, but we only gained it by a sturdy perseverance, coupled with patience and courteous candour. Delays were caused by Japanese dilatoriness and Japanese provocations ; the Netherland position was always clearly—if not bluntly— stated. Nothing was done which, from our point of view, might not have been published straight away ; the Japanese wanted secrecy, for obvious reasons. Because of this we could not refute propaganda lies, or correct *bona-fide* mis-statements.

The same applies to the rather wild rumours that arose over the oil contracts. Again, the reader will see that the truth was much simpler than it appeared at the time. Our decisions had to be guided by various considerations, but those concerning our national security and the common war effort prevailed. The net results barely covered the requirements of two months' warfare for the Japanese.

If anything deserved special praise, it was the fortitude of the people in the face of increasingly threatening disaster. Like all peaceful democracies, we were caught insufficiently prepared. This book does not treat of military matters. Suffice it to say that the considerable rearmament projects voted shortly before the Second World War could not be executed because we lacked an adequate heavy industry, and the war almost closed the armaments markets to our low priority. What could be done, was done, and little though it was, it created a certain temporary optimism, which was still further strength-ened by the trend of policy in the United States. Those who possessed inside knowledge, however, realized the lack of concerted preparation, due to the plight of Britain in Europe and the legal and political obstacles to military commitments in Washington.

As the menace grew and the real state of things began to be more widely known, the optimism disappeared. Perhaps we in the Netherlands Indies were certain of a Japanese attack at an earlier date than others, because we could not rely on our military power to deter the aggressor. But the Government decision that there would be no evacuation of white people was not even questioned; it fully corresponded with the choice the Netherlanders in the Indies had long since made for themselves. In this country, which had become their home, they would stay and fight; they would not leave their Indonesian co-patriots and friends in times of danger.

When our women, with a slight tightening at the throat, gazed after the thousands of European and American evacuees, drifting past and through our harbours on their way to safety; when the Japanese war machine came rolling southward; when it was certain that reinforcements would not arrive in time and might not arrive for a long time to come, they could have lamented with Jeremiah : " As for us, our eyes as yet failed for our vain help : in our watching we have watched for a nation that could not save us." They did not so lament. They met the fate that overtook them unflinchingly, fighting and staying on. And remember that they could have few illusions about what was in store for them under Japanese occupation.

The world has almost forgotten those fifty thousand Netherlanders in war prisons and internment camps, and the hundred thousand women and children, despoiled and destitute, living poorly in cramped segregation quarters or in other concentration wards. For nearly twenty months they hardly heard an Allied voice; only few of them may have seen an Allied plane in the sky. But we know—and this is no conjecture—that they do not despair; that they are standing by one another and have preserved their trust in ultimate victory ; that they feel their obligations towards the Indies and the Indonesians deeper than ever before. To the memory of those who died fighting, and the redemption of those who stayed on unbroken, may this book be dedicated.

H. J. van Mook.

London, 4th October 1943.

TABLE OF CONTENTS

CHAPTER I

BACKGROUND

It will not be possible to write the complete history of the relations between the Netherlands Indies and Japan, and of the growth and the frustration of Japanese ambitions in South-East Asia, until the Empire of the Rising Sun has been defeated and compelled to give up the secrets of those long years of planning and preparation which preceded Pearl Harbour. Facts and events have established the conviction that underneath and behind the stage upon which the pre-war drama of negotiations, pacts, and embargoes was presented, the plans of campaign and the armaments for outright aggression were being prepared and amassed without pause. But we cannot yet determine at what time the dreams of a number of ultra-nationalists became the aims of organized political and military groups; when those aims were incorporated in the policy of the Japanese Government; and on what occasion that Government decided the time had come for execution.

We may, however, assume that the subjection of South-East Asia under the direct rule or the supreme leadership of Japan has been the ultimate objective of Japanese policy for a much longer time than was generally understood. The slowly and deliberately moving Japanese temperament could not have planned the successful campaigns in the Philippines, Malaya, the Netherlands Indies, and Burma in a few months, nor even in a few years. What often has been described—mainly by Japanese diplomats who wanted to scare their opponents into peaceful submission—as a series of struggles between the peace and war parties in Tokyo, was as a rule only an ever-shifting conflict about the most promising ways

2

and means, or about the opportunities of the moment. Even peaceful, widely travelled, and " liberal " Japanese business-men were convinced, in their heart of hearts, that Japan could and should claim, as of right, a dominating position in South-East Asia. They might be doubtful about the prospects of a forcible assertion of that right, but they did not hesitate to consider any other independent force in that part of the world as a usurper. For in Japanese political philosophy preponderance must needs find expression in a right to command, in that " special position " which is so dear to the minds of their statesmen and soldiers.

If Japanese policy was constantly directed towards the acquisition of political and military hegemony in East and South-East Asia, the attitude of the neighbouring countries could only be one of unremitting vigilance, concentrating on defence and the avoidance of provocation. In the world of 1939-1941 combined resistance against aggression was but a slowly evolving idea ; the concept of the United Nations had not yet been born. China was fighting a lone fight ; the position of Russia was far from clear up to the middle of 1941 ; the United States was on the side of the Axis' victims, but only as a non-belligerent.

Still, there could be no compromise. Any concession would only serve to whet Japan's appetite and to weaken the power of resistance of the other party. The subsequent events have shown that the only thing to be gained was time, and time could best be gained by a course of action that neither forced not strengthened the hand of Japan.

The development of relations between Japan and the Netherlands, and more particularly the Netherlands Indies, from the beginning of 1940 until war broke out in December 1941, can only be judged fairly if we never lose sight of the gradual but fundamental changes in the international align-ment during the period. It was a minor scene in the fateful drama of the Second World War. Its importance, though not decisive, may be estimated if we speculate upon what would have happened, had the Netherlands Indies succumbed to Japanese pressure in the same way as Indo-China. The story illustrates how a policy may derive strength, in extremely difficult circumstances, from the adherence to clear and reasonable principles.

The facts can be published without reserve on the part of the Netherlands and the Netherland Indies. During the several contacts and negotiations in those years no essential fact or viewpoint was withheld from the Japanese ; none need remain hidden from the general public, now that Japan has forfeited any claim to discretion by her wanton attack.

The Japanese were convinced throughout that the actions and refusals of the Netherland and the Netherlands Indies Government were dictated by London and Washington. It was impossible for them to believe that a " colony," especially after the mother-country had been invaded and occupied by the enemy, could have the moral force to stand up against their blandishments and their veiled threats without the certainty of a substantial backing by great Powers. And as such backing, in their understanding, could only have been promised on the condition of strict obedience to orders, their conclusion seemed inevitable.

Anybody with a more than superficial knowledge of international relations and commitments during those years must realize that the facts were quite different. The Netherlands Indies, far from being the cowed and quasi neutral " colony " of Japanese imagination, were a largely self-governing partner in the Kingdom of the Netherlands ; under the supervision and guidance of Her Majesty's Government in London they were heart and soul in the war against Germany since the brutal assault of 10th May 1940. The British Empire, being almost alone in bearing the brunt of Axis attacks, could not be expected to divert a considerable part of its forces towards the Pacific. In the United States public opinion was in a flux and had not yet by any means been crystallized on armed participation in the war.

Therefore the Netherland Government and the Netherlands Indies, for the time being, had to fend for themselves in their dealings with Japan. In one respect, of course, there was close co-operation with our great British ally : the blockade of the Axis Powers had to be maintained as strictly as possible. Apart from that there was no consultation and no concerted action, although the Netherland Government kept the British and the United States Governments fully informed. This was an obvious necessity because of the interrelation of policies in the Pacific. Experience has shown that lack of mutual frankness with regard to matters of identical interest can only lead to misunderstandings and disagreeable surprises. When the Japanese objected, the obvious retort was that the Netherland Government must retain their freedom in this respect and that they, from their side, made no inquiries concerning possible communications between Tokyo and Berlin.

In the following narrative the principal documents are given in their full original text—as far as they were in English —or in an accurate translation. It seemed better to err on the side of circumstantiality, than to create the impression of reticence. Errors in grammar, idiom, and orthography are copied from the originals, which were written in a language foreign to both parties.

CHAPTER II

RELATIONS BEFORE 1940

RELATIONS between the Netherlands Indies and Japan presented no special difficulties until after the world crisis of 1929. In 1899 a law had accorded the Japanese the status of "Europeans" in the Indies; in 1912 a general trade treaty had put their activities in that country with regard to trade, business, shipping, and immigration on the normal footing of a most-favoured nation clause.

The Japanese were late in the business field; their participation in tropical agriculture and mining remained very limited, not because of any opposition, but because others had got the start of them. In imports and exports, banking and shipping their share was better and gradually increasing, but until about 1929 there were no disturbing developments.

When the world economic crisis began, this situation changed rapidly and materially. Japan's share in Netherlands Indies' imports rose from 11 per cent. in 1929 to 30 per cent. in 1935, whereas in the same period those percentages for the Netherlands, the rest of Europe, and America dropped from 20 to 13, from 28 to 23, and from 13 to 8 respectively. At the same time the share of Japan in the Netherlands Indies' exports was only 5 per cent. in 1935, as against 22, 18, and 15 per cent. for the Netherlands, Europe, and America. In a world where bilateralism in trade relations gained more ground every year, this created an impossible situation for a country dependent on exports to such an extent as the Netherlands Indies. Even the fact that cheap Japanese goods for mass consumption were in themselves a boon for the crisis-stricken population could not compensate the threatening loss of export markets.

But if this change in the balance of trade was the most

spectacular result of the crisis, the accompanying phenomena raised even graver apprehensions. As Japanese imports increased in volume, an objectionable characteristic of Japanese business outside Japan was disproportionately intensified. The Nippon emigrant has a tendency to isolate himself and his business from the community whose hospitality he enjoys. He likes to create, as it were, a Japanese enclave in the country and tries to extend his activity, as much as possible, with the help of his own countrymen. Although every foreign community tends to form a separate group, there is generally a gradual merging of the foreign settlers with elements of the local population ; in the case of the Japanese, however, these colonies sometimes remain indigestible units in almost every respect.

Moreover, as their numbers grow they endeavour rather to lessen than to multiply the contracts with the people and the institutions of the country in which they are living. They not only want their own clubs, societies, and places of worship, but also their own schools, doctors, and dentists, their own banks, shops, and means of transport, their own periodicals and printing presses. If they have their way, they will recruit nothing from the local population but labour ; the whole staff and—if possible—all the foremen must be Japanese. They look upon their trade, their plantations, their mines, and their factories in foreign countries as integrated parts of the economy of the Japanese Empire. If they were allowed to do so they would instal their own policemen and their own magistrates. In short, the extra-territorial rights which they strove so hard to abolish in their own country during the last decades of the nineteenth century, would precisely fit the needs and ambitions of Japanese communities abroad.

Insularity of character and linguistic incapacity are but a partial explanation of this trait. Ingrained in their minds is the conviction that Japanese, wherever they reside, should be governed exclusively by authorities deriving their power from the deified Emperor. This conviction makes them ideal agents for an expansionist policy. It creates the opportunity of a combination of ordinary business with political activity on a large scale, which sometimes may look childish in the individual case, but which provides Japan with a comprehensive and efficient machinery for collecting data and preparing her advances.

The earlier Japanese investments in the Netherlands Indies may have been of a more purely private character, with some occasional spying thrown in; in the 'thirties penetration became definitely organized, and was pushed from behind by those semi-official, Government-subsidized corporations like the Nanyo Kohatsu, whose ultimate aims were revealed by naval and military participation. The rising flood of imports carried Japanese goods of Japanese importers in Japanese ships, financed by Japanese banks, to Japanese warehouses in the coastal towns of Java, to be sold directly to the consumers through Japanese retailers far in the interior. Japanese middlemen penetrated in East Java, South-East Borneo, and North Celebes to buy native products—maize, rubber, and copra—for export to Japan. Japanese fisheries started operations in the strategically important seas North of Batavia and around the Northern peninsula of Celebes, continually trespassing into territorial waters and causing several incidents. Mining, agricultural, and lumber rights, mostly of doubtful economic value, were bought or applied for in localities of military importance, e.g. the East and West coasts of Borneo and the Northern part of New Guinea. Small craft began to penetrate into coastal shipping.

In the beginning it was difficult to piece together this whole connected movement from the apparently disconnected moves, as it was difficult to distinguish the professional soldiers and spies among the growing multitude of merchants, planters, and fishermen. In the meantime another danger became evident. The Indonesian inhabitants of the Indies were beginning to reach a level of education which would enable them to enter staff positions in modern business, or to modernize and expand their own industries. But to achieve this successfully in the years of apprenticeship and initial experiment they needed room for development. Unlimited admittance of the experienced and low-salaried Japanese, with their preference for wholly Japanese personnel, would have put another obstacle in the way of Indonesian emancipation, and would have crowded out the budding Indonesian entrepreneur.

Lastly, Japanese war economy was taking a direction which made Japan a worse customer for the Netherlands Indies every year. Her need for armaments and her lack of exchange made her prefer low grade raw materials to high grade, crude to refined products, expensive home-grown commodities to cheap imports, guns to sugar. This trend became very clear after the outbreak of the war in China, but it was already noticeable at the time of the Manchurian " incident." The export of sugar from the Netherlands Indies to Japan fell from 200,000 tons in 1936 to 500 tons in 1939 ; the export of tapioca from 43,000 tons in 1936 to 2,500 tons in 1939 ; the export of mineral oil products from 927,000 tons in 1937 to 547,000 tons in 1939 ; the export of lumber from 85,000 cubic metres in 1936 to 54,000 cubic metres in 1939. Japan was fast becoming a negligible factor in the creation of international purchasing power for the Netherlands Indies, and a definite obstacle for the development of primary industries in that country.

To fend off these dangers and to restore such gradualness in the course of events as was needed to maintain harmonious international relations, a number of protective measures were introduced in those years of crisis. These measures were of a general character ; neither in their provisions, nor in their execution was there any discrimination against Japan. If, nevertheless, they were decried in Tokyo as the instruments of an anti-Japanese policy, this view was caused by the fact that they effectively blocked the efforts of Japan to create for herself a special and dominating position in the Indies.

Those measures mainly comprised the following items. A licensing law for imports and import business, affecting about one-fourth of the total imports, put a generous limit to Japanese expansion in this field, safeguarded existing business concerns, provided import quota for our best customers, and at the same time left the entrance free for cheap articles of mass consumption. Incidentally it gave some protection to the growing industry, which could not shelter behind the purely fiscal tariff. A law on foreign labour protected the local labour market against unwarranted admittance of foreign workers and employees. A law for the regulation of trades made it possible to bring certain branches of industry under a licensing system, to direct their growth, and to prevent cut-throat competition. The introduction of immigration quota provided a very necessary limitation of the annual number of immigrants into a country, where the island of Java has over 900 inhabitants to the square mile.[1] A shipping law designated the ports open to international shipping, and reserved coasting trade to vessels under the Netherland flag, while allowing the continuation of the few foreign services—British and Japanese—already established. A law on marine fisheries prohibited foreign fishing in territorial waters.

When most of these measures still were in preparation, Japan protested and the first formal economic negotiations were opened. The two delegations met at Batavia in the middle of 1934.[2] The often rather heated discussions were protracted until the end of the year, but the situation was impossible, as the Netherlands Indies Government had already decided to put the projected measures into effect ; our delegation had nothing to offer but restrictions.

[1] As against 3 in Canada and 43 in the United States.
[2] Chairman of the Netherland delegation was Dr. J. W. Meyer Ranneft, Vice-President of the Council of the Netherlands Indies ; their leading spirit was the late Professor J. van Gelderen. The Japanese delegation was led by Ambassador Nagaoka.

However, the negotiations did not prove wholly abortive. After the Japanese delegation had left, the discussions were continued between the Director of Economic Affairs [1] and the Japanese Consul-General.[2]   In 1937 an agreement was reached after the legislation, mentioned before, had been put into force and economic relations had been more or less stabilized. In the Hart-Ishizawa agreement Japan accepted the new situation and the Netherlands agreed to maintain the Japanese position on the reduced level ; Japan's share in the Netherlands Indies' imports meanwhile had fallen to 15 per cent. Both parties undertook to promote mutual trade ; Japan particularly agreed to promote increased purchases of products like sugar, coffee, copra, and kapok, all of them important factors in Indonesian economy.

The agreement was supplemented in 1938 by the Van Mook-Kotani agreement [3] regulating the position of Netherland merchants in Japan, which had been adversely affected by the establishment of exporters' associations by the Japanese Government.   The shipping situation had already been eased by the conclusion of a pooling agreement between the companies concerned in 1936, which was acknowledged by the respective Governments.

It is difficult to determine whether the rapid deterioration of Netherlands Indies' exports to Japan since 1937, mention of which was made before, was caused by the war in China alone or whether it was the result of a more fundamental and preconceived policy.   The fact remains that the balance of trade became ever more unsatisfactory for the Netherlands Indies.   To this were added the vexations and losses resulting from Japanese action and depredations in China.   Although Japan never asked the Netherland Government to recognize the Nanking puppet regime, the war in China caused many

---

[1] Dr. G. H. C. Hart ; " director " in the Netherlands Indies is the head of a civil department.   [2] Mr. Y. Ishizawa.
[3] Initialled by Mr. H. J. van Mook, Director of Economic Affairs since September 1937, and Mr. Kotani, acting Consul-General.

minor disagreements. Public opinion in the Indies was solidly on the Chungking side, and although public collections of money and materials were strictly limited to Red Cross purposes, demonstrations of sympathy could not always be checked or prevented.[1] Notwithstanding all these difficulties relations remained tolerably good until the Second World War broke out in September 1939.

[1] Curiously enough Japan never objected to the continuation of remittances of the Chinese in the Netherlands Indies to their families in South China, totalling over two million guilders a month, which were a definite asset in relieving Chungking's exchange difficulties.

CHAPTER III

THE OPENING MOVES

THE first indication of a changing attitude in Tokyo came on 2nd February 1940, when the Japanese Government, through their Minister at The Hague, requested the Netherland Government to enter into discussions on the subject of trade between Japan and the Netherlands Indies and on that of the position of Japanese and Netherland subjects in the Netherlands Indies and Japan, respectively. Mr. Ishii handed a sketchy note to Dr. E. N. van Kleffens, Netherland Minister of Foreign Affairs, containing a number of demands and offers and drawn up in what might appear to be a scrupulously reciprocal manner. But those familiar with the facts and their history could perceive at first glance how much the dice were loaded on the Japanese side. The note, which had an unusual appearance and which was presented in a slightly different wording to the Netherland Minister at Tokyo on 8th March, read as follows :

> Note handed by Mr. Ishii, Japanese Minister at The Hague, to Dr. Van Kleffens, Netherland Minister of Foreign Affairs, on the 2nd of February, 1940.

> Chief items desired to be agreed upon between Japan and the Netherlands.

I. MATTERS RELATING TO COMMERCE.

  (1) Japanese Side :

    (*a*) Japan is to refrain, as far as circumstances permit, from adopting any measure prohibiting or restricting the exportation of its principal goods required by the Netherlands Indies. (It is to be understood that the exportation may sometimes be difficult for economic reasons.)

(b) Japan is to adopt such measures as deemed to be appropriate with a view to furthering the importation of goods from the Netherlands Indies.

(2) Netherlands Side :

(a) The Netherlands Indies is likewise to refrain from adopting any measure prohibiting or restricting the exportation of its principal goods ; the prohibitive or restrictive measures, to which the exportation of certain goods has already been subjected are to be so modified as to render the flow of goods easier between Japan and the Netherlands Indies.

(b) The existing measures of import restrictions in respect of Japanese goods are to be abolished or moderated.

II. MATTERS RELATING TO ENTRY.

(1) Japanese Side :

Japan is, as at present, to adopt no restrictive measures in future in respect of the entry of employees of Netherlands firms in Japan.

(2) Netherlands Side :

The existing Foreigners Labour Ordinance in the Netherlands Indies is to be abolished or moderated.

III. MATTERS RELATING TO ENTERPRISE AND INVESTMENT.

(1) Japanese Side :

(a) Japan is to afford, within its influence and competence, reasonable protection to Netherlands interests in Manchukuo and China.

(b) Facilities are to be afforded in respect of new Netherlands investments in Japan ; its offer of investment to Manchukuo and China is to be recommended by Japan to be accommodated, to the governments concerned.

(2) Netherlands Side :

(a) Further facilities are to be extended to the existing Japanese enterprises in the Netherlands Indies.

(b) Facilities are to be granted to new enterprises, including those under joint control of Japan and the Netherlands.

IV. CONTROL OF PRESS AND OTHER PUBLICATIONS OF ANTI-JAPANESE NATURE.

The anti-Netherlands tendency, if any, of the Press, magazines and other publications in Japan on one hand, and the anti-Japanese tendency of the Press, magazines and other publications in Netherlands and the Netherlands Indies on the other, are to be placed respectively under strict control in conformity with friendly spirit prevailing between Japan and the Netherlands.

During the resulting conversation Mr. Ishii suggested negotiations at The Hague and promised more detailed propositions to follow. It is noteworthy that Japan not only grasped the opportunity, provided by the circumstances of war, to renew her attempts at a more privileged position, but that she also showed concern about her access to raw materials at this early date. At the time she bought less oil in the Netherlands Indies than had been the case for many years ; the bulk of her rubber and tin requirements were still purchased in Malaya. Exports from the Netherlands Indies were regulated in order to prevent difficulties with the nations then at war, but they were not otherwise restricted ; a few measures taken to ensure the availability of foodstuffs and raw materials for home consumption in the Netherlands Indies themselves could hardly affect the interests of Japan. But the British Empire was at war, and the trade treaty between Japan and the United States had expired in January. The war machine in Tokyo did not lack foresight.

A suitable reply was still under consideration when, on the 10th of May 1940, the Netherlands were attacked and invaded by Germany.

It is difficult, at this juncture and after so many terrible developments, to reconstruct the shock caused in the Netherlands Indies by this wholly unwarranted attack and the subsequent events. Although the Government had taken all necessary steps to cope with the emergencies that would result from German aggression, and although the conviction had gradually taken root that the Nazis would stop at nothing— as had been proved in Denmark and Norway, the month before —the sudden and overwhelming nature of the assault, for the moment, had a numbing effect on public opinion. The Government acted promptly ; within twelve hours after the attack eighteen out of nineteen German merchantmen in our harbours had been captured,[1] and all Germans had been rounded up and interned. During the following weeks the whole organization of business and trade had to be overhauled in order to repair the damage caused by the sudden occupation of the mother-country, and stringent measures were put through to bring the Indies on a war footing.   The first mood of impotent rage quickly gave way to one of grim determination, but one can easily imagine the violent disturbance of those initial weeks of war.

When the Netherlands were invaded, Japan acted with perfectly indecent speed. On 14th May, when the centre of Rotterdam had been blasted out of existence and the Netherland Government had moved to London, the Japanese Minister at The Hague presented a memorandum at the Netherland Ministry of Foreign Affairs, picking his way through parachutists and street fighting. On 18th May the Japanese Consul-General at Batavia delivered condolences, requests, and veiled threats almost in one and the same breath. On 20th May Foreign Minister Arita handed a note to the Netherland Minister in Tokyo of the following contents :

Note handed to the Netherland Minister in Japan, General J. C. Pabst, by the Japanese Foreign Minister, Mr. Arita, on the 20th of May, 1940.

I have the honour to refer to my conversation with Your Excellency on the 16th May concerning the products of the Netherlands East Indies, in the course of which you informed me that you had received a telegram from the Governor-General of the Netherlands East Indies to the effect that the Government-General of the Netherlands East Indies had no intention of placing any restrictions in future on the exportation to Japan of mineral oil, tin, rubber, and other raw materials which are of vital importance to Japan, and that it was the desire of the same Government-General to maintain

[1] Only one was sunk by her crew ; she was lying four miles out because of a cargo of explosives, which gave the people on board the opportunity to forestall seizure.

the general economic relations between Japan and the Netherlands East Indies as close as ever.

While informing Your Excellency that the Japanese Government fully appreciate the communication of the Government-General of the Netherlands East Indies, I wish to point out that, in addition to mineral oil, tin, and rubber, there are many other kinds of commodities hitherto imported into Japan from the Netherlands East Indies which are of vital importance to this country.

It is, therefore, requested that the Government-General of the Netherlands East Indies would give a definite assurance that, for the time being, at least, the quantities of the articles enumerated in the attached list shall be exported to Japan each year from the Netherlands East Indies under any circumstances that may arise in future.

In view of the above-mentioned telegraphic communication from the Governor-General of the Netherlands East Indies and of the wide powers with which he has been vested since the outbreak of hostilities between the Netherlands and Germany (*vide* Your Excellency's note addressed to me under date of the 11th May), I shall be grateful if Your Excellency will be good enough to inform me in writing as soon as possible that the Governor-General of the Netherlands East Indies accedes to the above-mentioned request of the Japanese Government.

1. Tin (including ore) 3,000 tons
2. Rubber 20,000 tons
3. Mineral oil 1,000,000 tons
4. Bauxite 200,000 tons
5. Nickel ore 150,000 tons
6. Manganese ore 50,000 tons
7. Wolfram 1,000 tons
8. Scrap-iron 100,000 tons
9. Chrome iron ore 5,000 tons
10. Salt 100,000 tons
11. Castor seeds 4,000 tons
12. Quinine bark 600 tons
13. Molybdenum 1,000 tons

The reference to the wide powers accorded to the Governor-General of the Netherlands Indies, was based on the erroneous interpretation of certain emergency instructions which did not come into force because the Netherland Government had removed their seat to London in time to retain their freedom of action. But one can understand the difficulties caused by this Japanese move at a time when the Netherland Government had to cope with all the problems of setting up new headquarters in a foreign—though allied

and hospitable—country. The situation was still further
complicated by the fact that the Japanese Government failed
to appoint a representative at Her Majesty's court in London,
so that oral discussion could only take place in Tokyo and,
to a certain extent, in Batavia.

The Netherlands Indies, where the Government had to
be fully consulted, were at the moment like a house which
has had part of its roof blown off in a storm. Everybody
was working sixteen hours a day to reconstruct the roof
when Japan pounded the door and asked the inhabitants
to stand and deliver. On 28th May Tokyo again insisted on
a speedy reply and on immediate negotiations at Batavia,
because otherwise the Japanese extremists would become
uncontrollable and endanger the position of the existing
Cabinet. It took some time to formulate the answer ; on
the 6th of June it was handed to the Japanese Government.

Note addressed to Mr. H. Arita, Japanese Minister
of Foreign Affairs, by the Netherland Minister in
Tokyo on 6th June 1940.
(Translation from the original in French.)

With reference to the correspondence between the Netherland
Government and the Japanese Government on the subject of the
improvement of the economic relations between the two countries,
I have the honour to inform Your Excellency that the Netherland
Government highly appreciate the Japanese Government's ex-
pression of sympathy with the difficult situation in which the
Netherlands find themselves as a consequence of the war. My
Government, moreover, appreciate that the memorandum, which
was to be presented by the Japanese Minister at The Hague, and
which was on the 18th of May 1940 presented to the Governor-
General of the Netherlands Indies by the Japanese Consul-General
at Batavia, as further amplified by Your Excellency's note dated
May 20th 1940, No. 1006, was clearly actuated by concern, lest,
in these difficult times, a lack of contact and deliberation should
give rise to or protract tensions to the detriment of the traditional
friendly relations which, for three centuries, so fortunately prevailed between the Netherlands and Japan. The Netherland
Government agree with the Japanese Government on the necessity

of combating incorrect reports and mis-directed propaganda. This aim will be best furthered by contacts made in an atmosphere of frankness and objectivity.

Her Majesty's Government see no cause whatsoever for serious concern about the relations between the Netherlands and Japan and, more particularly, about the relations between the Netherlands Indies and Japan.

In this respect it may serve to recall that the economic relations between the two countries were settled on the 9th of April 1937 by the so-called Hart-Ishizawa agreement. On both sides promises were made, and a number of apportionments were agreed upon, whilst on other points and on the subject of the application of the agreement, verbal as well as written negotiations were continuously carried on. Throughout these deliberations a spirit of goodwill predominated. I may, for instance, mention that in 1938 the Netherland Government thought fit to draw the attention of the Japanese Government to the fact that the prospects opened by the Hart-Ishizawa agreement in respect of the gradual adjustment of the balance of trade between the Netherlands Indies and Japan and of Japan's promise to buy, whenever possible, larger quantities of indigenous products like sugar, still fell far short of their realization. This step was dictated by the fundamental importance of these exports for the native population. The importation of many Japanese articles has its foundation in the purchasing power of this population.

Notwithstanding this none too satisfactory outcome for the Netherland Government, my Government have accepted the explanation given by the Japanese Government that the China incident had a considerable influence on economic conditions in Japan, as well as on the fulfilment of this part of the Hart-Ishizawa agreement. In judging the results realized through the Hart-Ishizawa agreement, the Netherland Government have always given due consideration to those exigencies, which are the inevitable consequence of war conditions. The Netherland Government, therefore, are convinced that the fact that they, too, were forced into war, will have the Japanese Government's consideration. This state of war must, of necessity, have its repercussions on the economic situation in the Netherlands Indies.

In any case, my Government fully well understand that it is important for Japan as well as for the Netherlands Indies that the commercial relations between the two countries develop without hindrance.

With satisfaction the Netherland Government have taken notice of Your Excellency's statements concerning the importance of maintaining the *status quo* of the Netherlands Indies. Repeatedly my Government have confirmed that they wish to maintain this *status quo* without reserve. This mutual declaration is considered the more important, since the maintenance of the *status quo* bears closely upon the interests of their Allies as well as upon those of other countries bordering upon the Pacific, as is clearly evidenced by the statements made by Great Britain, France, and the United States of America.

It is, in fact, of great importance for the maintenance of peace in this part of the world that the position of the Netherlands Indies remain unimpaired, and that this country be able to continue without interruption to act its part as a world-supplier of various raw materials and food products.

I may now be allowed to give a reply to Your Excellency on the proposals contained in the note of the Japanese Minister at The Hague of February 2nd 1940, and in the above-mentioned memorandum, as further amplified by Your Excellency's note.

COMMERCIAL RELATIONS BETWEEN THE NETHERLANDS INDIES AND JAPAN.

The Governments of the Netherlands and of the Netherlands Indies have already declared that they in no way intend to restrict the trade between the Netherlands Indies and Japan. On the contrary, the progressive development of the commercial relations is just as important to the Netherlands Indies as to Japan. The more so, since the income derived from export is, in these times of changed international relations, even more than previously of vital importance for the population of the Netherlands Indies, who can only afford to buy import goods of prime necessity if the exports provide them with the means thereto. The more it may prove possible to adjust the balance of trade, which these last years was pronouncedly negative, the more it will be possible to give added encouragement to the importation of Japanese products. Since the Netherland Government have in the past consistently tried to stimulate the export to Japan, they have no objection whatsoever once more to give the assurance, for which the Japanese Government have asked, that the Netherland Government as well as the Netherlands Indies Government will refrain from taking measures which might hamper the exportation of the 13 mentioned products in their equally mentioned quantities. In order to avoid any possible misunderstanding concerning these quantities, Your Excellency will find enclosed an explanatory note on the subject.

To the preceding should be added, in conformity with previous statements, that the change in the international conditions first of all demands that the Netherlands Indies introduce regulations for exchange-control. The Imperial Government will understand that such measures are unavoidable, amongst other things in order to maintain the rates of exchange with the yen and the dollar. It is further necessary to take measures to prevent that the products exported by the Netherlands Indies should ultimately fall into the hands of the enemy, and to prevent that excessive exports should cause want in the Netherlands Indies themselves. In taking these measures a method of execution will be sought, calculated to minimize harmful effects to the normal commercial intercourse with foreign countries. The importation of merchandise of Japanese origin, which formed the subject of searching deliberations, leading to identical viewpoints in the Hart-Ishizawa agreement, will be continued in the normal way. In view of the existing conditions, there is reason to expect that the imports will tend to increase rather than to diminish.

The Royal Government do not lose sight of the fact that present events necessarily require a modified application of the existing import regulations. In their judgment, however, the basic value of these regulations has remained unchanged.

As already stated : the possibility to import is the direct complement of the possibility to export. Anything harmful to these exports will, therefore, be as detrimental to Japan as to the Netherlands Indies. Thence a policy of adjustment of the balance of trade will be followed. Intensified exports to Japan, and the resumption of the exportation of those products which best serve to stimulate the purchasing power of the native population (sugar, copra, kapok, coffee, palmoil, tobacco, maize, wood, damar, copal and other resinous products, and rattan) could especially contribute to the maintenance and growth of import possibilities.

With satisfaction the Netherland Government have taken cognizance of the Japanese Government's intention to refrain as much as possible from taking prohibitive or restrictive measures with regard to articles needed by the Netherlands Indies. They have also taken note of the reservations in case of shortage of raw materials or fuel.

The Japanese Government suggested that positive measures should be taken to stimulate the importation of indigenous products. This suggestion has been fully appreciated, and the Royal Government hope that these measures will contribute towards restoring or improving the importation of the products specifically enumerated in the Hart-Ishizawa agreement.

IMMIGRATION.

The Netherland Government regret that they cannot see their way to revoke the ordinance regulating the labour-permits for foreigners. This ordinance constitutes a necessary measure for the protection of labour in the Indies, particularly with regard to the more advanced Indonesians, the Europeans, and the non-indigenous orientals born in the Indies. If this ordinance were revoked, the result would be an influx of all sorts of foreigners, and this would seriously affect the occupational possibilities of the afore-mentioned categories. It is evident that a partial revocation applying to a single country is out of question, since such a measure would be in contradiction with the traditional policy of the Netherland Government, which implies equal treatment of all nationalities. A measure of this kind would mean a violation of the desired *status quo*.

The Netherland Government are of the opinion that the requests of Japanese individuals have been treated with great consideration and that not a single case occurred of an employer meeting with a refusal after he had proved the necessity of obtaining a permit. The Netherland Government will continue to follow this policy and are convinced that the Japanese Government, with a full understanding of the necessity of these measures, will for the future entertain no fear of any serious difficulty for her nationals.

My Government appreciate that in Japan no restrictions are imposed on the immigration of Netherland merchants and business-employees. However, one has to take into consideration the very restricted number of Netherland nationals in Japan, as well as the fact that the merchants concerned employ mostly Japanese labour.

BUSINESS CONCERNS AND CAPITAL INVESTMENT.

The Netherland Government wish to draw attention to the fact that in the Netherlands Indies a liberal policy is followed in respect of the establishment of commercial enterprises and the investment of capital by foreigners.

This policy found expression in the Commercial Treaty concluded between the Netherlands and Japan in 1912. The Government have not imposed any conditions or restrictive measures, except where the interests of the population of the Netherlands Indies or the vital interests of the Kingdom demanded such action, which was then taken without in any way discriminating between countries. My Government consider this policy so equitable and well justified as to deserve to be maintained for the future. For previously stated reasons it is not possible to make an exception for a separate country. With regard to isolated cases, the Royal Government have to draw the Imperial Government's attention to the fact that the initiative is left to the individual merchant, equally so where mixed Netherlands-Japanese undertakings are concerned. For reasons of public safety the Government reserve their right to exploit certain enterprises themselves.

The Netherland Government take for granted that the Netherland interests in Japan, in China and in Manchuria are fully protected, just as the Japanese interests in the Indies enjoy the full protection of the Netherland Government. The prospect of facilities for investment held out by the Japanese Government is appreciated by the Netherland Government, although for the present they regard the interest which such investments would have for their nationals as rather limited.

CONTROL OF THE PRESS.

As the Japanese Government know, the Netherlands Indies' authorities keep a close watch on the press in order to hold in check the publication of articles which manifest an undesirable attitude towards foreign powers. It may serve a useful purpose to report that, thanks to this supervision, repercussions in the Netherlands Indies of events in China were limited and never, not even temporarily, assumed a serious character. Under the present circumstances this control is being applied even more rigorously.

The Netherland Government believe that their line of conduct leaves no room for any fear that the good relations might become endangered through the activities of the Press.

On the strength of the above arguments the Netherland Government believe that the treaties now in force, together with the practice of existing relations, satisfactorily express the principles and the fundamentals on which the good relations between the Netherlands and Japan may remain based, in particular where the economic relations between the Netherlands Indies and Japan are concerned.

The Royal Government flatter themselves with the belief that the preceding supplies a satisfactory explanation on those points, concerning which the Japanese Government might entertain some doubts. It is possible, however, that specific questions may occasionally arise concerning definite subjects, which have a bearing on the economic relations between the Netherlands Indies and Japan. In such cases the point at issue could be discussed and arranged between the Japanese Consul-General in Batavia and the authorities designated by the Government of the Netherlands Indies. The Netherland Government believe that in most cases these questions can be solved in this manner.

Appendix

Some observations on the 13 export products, mentioned in the note from the Japanese Consul-General in Batavia to the Governor-General of the Netherlands Indies, dated May 18th, 1940, and in the note of His Excellency Mr. Hachiro Arita which was handed to the Netherlands Minister at Tokyo on May 20th, 1940.

The figures referring to

> bauxite (200,000 tons)
> chrome-iron ore (5,000 tons)
> nickel ore (150,000 tons)
> tin and tin ore (3,000 tons)
> rubber (20,000 tons)
> cinchona bark (600 tons)
> ricinus seeds (4,000 tons)

do not give rise to any observations.

The figure for petroleum-products (1,000,000 tons) is considerably higher than the average export from the Netherlands Indies to Japan during the last three years. The export was in

> 1937   869,000 tons
> 1938   668,000 tons
> 1939   573,000 tons

The oil companies in the Netherlands Indies may be able to supply the required quantities, provided the Japanese, on their part, conclude the contracts in time.

It is possible to produce a quantity of 100,000 tons of salt, provided a contract is concluded for several years, since it will be necessary to put new salt-works into operation. The salt production in the Netherlands Indies is intended exclusively for the home market, whilst the reserves are almost exhausted owing to unfavourable atmospheric conditions. Normally it will not be possible to start deliveries before November 1940. It might be possible to advance this date if a contract can be concluded for several years. This would ensure the supply of the necessary reserves.

The figure for scrap-iron (100,000 tons) is in excess of the quantity annually available for export. In 1937 the export amounted to 103,700 tons, in 1938 to 60,600 tons, and in 1939 to 47,200 tons, which quantities were exported almost exclusively to Japan. We are willing to guarantee that the export to Japan of the quantities of scrap-iron available for export will not be subject to any restrictions.

It is apparent that the figure for manganese ore (50,000 tons) cannot be correct. The total exports, which represented almost the entire output, amounted in 1937 to 15,700 tons, in 1938 to 11,200 tons, and in 1939 to 7,300 tons. Of these quantities almost nothing was bought by Japan. Apart from the mines at present under exploitation, we do not know of the existence of any other important strata. In so far as the contracts under execution permit, Japan can freely buy this product.

The figures for wolfram and for molybdenum (1,000 tons) are not in accordance with production figures. Wolfram is obtained only in very small quantities through the exploitation of tin. These quantities, amounting to at most a few tons a year, were always exported to Japan. There never has been any export of molybdenum. It is but rarely found in the Netherlands Indies.

It had to be a cautious answer. All the time the Government were framing it, the wave of German Blitzkrieg was rolling through Belgium and France. It was no time for complications in the Far East. Japan's requests with regard to exports, at that stage, were in themselves not unreasonable. Where the quantities named were not patently mistaken, they were near or sometimes even below the maximum annual exports in the recent past. Some reservation had to be made with regard to war conditions, but there had been hardly time enough to realize what war conditions might imply for the Netherlands Indies. When the Japanese Government asked, on the 28th of June, for a definite undertaking by the Netherland Government and the Governor-General to export annually to Japan, under any circumstances, at least the quantities mentioned in the first note, the answer given after serious consultation had to be still more cautious. The Netherland Government could only undertake to stimulate and to facilitate exports, as they were no exporters themselves ; they had to point out with regard to some of the materials that production was too low to provide the quantities asked. France had capitulated on the 22nd of June ; the Burma Road had been closed on 18th July ; there were indications of increasing pressure with regard to the closure of the Tongkin-Yunnan Road and to Japanese control in Northern Indo-China. On the other hand, the first measures to control and to limit the exports from the United States to Japan of mineral oil and oil products (particularly of aviation spirit) were taken during the last days of July. The Japanese promptly raised the figure of their annual oil requirements from the Netherlands Indies to 2,000,000 tons, but were referred to the oil-producing companies with which they would have to negotiate, as the governmental authority in this field did not include control of sales, except in connection with the exigencies of war.

There is no need to enlarge upon the statement, made by Minister Arita shortly after the occupation of the Netherlands, that the Japanese Government, from the standpoint of maintaining the peace and stability of East Asia, had a deep concern over any development that might affect the *status quo* of the Netherlands Indies. Its only significance was that it implied a presumption of Japanese leadership in East Asia, and that it disregarded the fact that the Netherlands Indies were at war.[1] The championing of peace and stability did not quite befit a power which had been causing war in East

[1] It is, perhaps, an interesting sidelight that Mr. Tani, Vice-Minister of Foreign Affairs, in a conversation with General Pabst, the Netherland Minister, shortly before the collapse of France, gave a new meaning to this *status quo* by declaring that Japan would not allow any change in the Netherlands Indies in case of a German victory and of more " intimate " relations between Germany and the Netherlands in consequence thereof.

Asia since 1931. In the subsequent proceedings there was once or twice a faint attempt to stigmatize war measures in the Netherlands Indies as changes of the *status quo*. Otherwise the declaration figured neither as an excuse for, nor as a deterrent from breaking the *status quo* altogether.

Before the related exchange of notes had reached its conclusion the Japanese Government repeated their proposals for negotiation on a more comprehensive scale. On the 16th of July they informed the Netherland Minister in Tokyo of their intention to send a delegation to Batavia for economic negotiations, under the chairmanship of Mr. Sako, ex-Ambassador in Poland, and comprising a number of assistants, military experts on war materials, oil experts, etc. The Consul-General in Batavia, Mr. O. Saito, a very aggressive and expansionist character, was to be included in the delegation.

Although the Netherland and the Netherlands Indies Government had objected to negotiations of a general or political nature, and did not see the need of such an elaborate machinery for the handling of special problems, it was deemed judicious not to oppose a stubborn refusal to the insistence of the Japanese Government. Negotiations, to be arranged in Batavia, were formally accepted on 1st August. On 2nd August the first batch of eight negotiators left Yokohama under the guise of private businessmen. Repeated efforts to obtain a clear statement of the subjects to be discussed failed to elicit anything definite, except the grudgingly given assurance that the negotiations would be limited to economic relations and the rather vague indication that the principal points to be raised by Japan would be the acquisition of oil and other raw materials, and the expansion of Japanese business and of the participation of Japan in the development of the Indies. A request to transfer Mr. Ishii, the Japanese Minister who had remained in Holland,[1] to London was denied under various excuses, and there was a recurrent and

---

[1] And might be studying the records of the Ministries of Foreign Affairs and of the Colonies with German assistance.

growing tendency on the Japanese side to try to eliminate the Netherland Government in London as much as possible from the proceedings ; a tendency which was as consistently combated from the Netherland side.

If the subject-matter of the proposed negotiations remained rather hazy, the question of personnel was very much in the foreground.   A change of Cabinet had led to the elimination of Mr. Sako.   In his place Mr. Sawada, ex-Ambassador in Brazil, was named as chief delegate, to be dropped again presently for General Koiso.   General Koiso, however, had given an interview to the Press on the 3rd of August, in which he had stated in rather violent terms that the Netherland regime always had been most oppressive towards the indigenous population of the Indies.   He could not, in the view of the Netherland Government, be acceptable as a delegate without at least a public retraction or denial of that statement.

While this question was still hanging fire, the Japanese Government suddenly, on the 27th of August, handed a memorandum to the Netherland Minister at Tokyo, begging to inform the Netherland Government that a special envoy to the Netherlands Indies had been appointed in the person of Mr. I. Kobayashi, Minister of Commerce and Industry in the Konoe cabinet.   He would be seconded in his mission to establish closer economic relations between the two countries by Mr. T. Ota, chief of section in the Gaimusho,[1] and by Mr. O. Saito, Japanese Consul-General in Batavia. They were to be accompanied by a staff of 24 assistants, including one Army, one Air, and two Naval officers.   This impressive company was to sail from Kobe on 31st August.

Much was made of the fact that Japan was sending a cabinet minister ; the Japanese Government intimated that Mr. Kobayashi was expected to discuss matters directly with the Governor-General to whom should be given wide powers of decision to expedite the negotiations.   The intention was easy to guess.   A cabinet minister and a governor-general

[1] The Japanese Foreign Office.

could not be expected to waste their valuable time in the discussion of technical economic adjustments; their rank and position would force the negotiations into the political enclosure. The governor-general of an " orphaned colony," cut off from the support of his Government and from the wicked interference of the British, could not be expected to stand up against the full force of Japanese Imperial power. The system had worked marvellously—with German aid— in Indo-China, but in the Indies a disappointment was inevitable. The Governor-General, who is the head of the Netherlands Indies Government, could not be expected to negotiate in person, and there was no reason for the Netherland Government in London to delegate exceptional powers in international affairs to the Government in Batavia.

They decided to appoint as chief delegate from their side Dr. Van Mook, Director of Economic Affairs; he was to be seconded by Dr. K. L. J. Enthoven, Director of Justice, and Raden L. Djajadiningrat, senior officer in the Department of Education, whereas Dr. J. E. van Hoogstraten, chief of the Bureau of Commerce, was to act as a general secretary of the Netherland delegation.[1] This decision met with grave objections in Tokyo; Dr. Van Mook was considered far too low in rank to oppose Mr. Kobayashi. As an ultimate concession the Netherland Government agreed to a strictly limited number of very general conversations between Mr. Kobayashi and the Governor-General, provided that in the actual negotiations his opposite number would be Dr. Van Mook, who was to be appointed Minister Plenipotentiary. While Mr. Kobayashi was sailing southward in blissful ignorance, the fight about the protocol continued to flash back and forth between London, Tokyo, and Batavia.

In the meantime the first set of actors had already arrived in Java. During the preceding months negotiations had

[1] The delegation was assisted throughout in a very capable manner by Mr. A. H. Lovink, Adviser for East Asiatic Affairs of the Government, and his staff.

been going on in several places and between several agencies
about the purchase of mineral oil and oil products from the
Netherlands Indies by Japan. In the last days of August
a party of eight Japanese gentlemen, headed by Mr. T. Mukai,
Chairman of the Board of Directors of the Mitsui concern,
arrived in Java with the purpose of continuing these negotiations. It soon transpired that they were to be attached to
the Kobayashi mission. As the Netherlands Indies Government from their side had urged the centralization of these
negotiations in Batavia, the principal oil-producing companies
had each sent one of their directors : J. C. van Panthaleon
Baron van Eck for the Royal Dutch-Shell group, and Mr.
Fred H. Kay for the Standard Vacuum group.

On the 12th of September the *Nissho Maru*, carrying the
Japanese delegation, entered Tandjong Priok harbour. The
ship was gaily hung with bunting, but the captain had forgotten to hoist the Netherland colours in the appropriate
place.

CHAPTER IV

THE KOBAYASHI MISSION

WHEN the Netherland delegation boarded the ship to welcome Mr. Kobayashi and his party, they did not know whether they would be met with an ultimatum, an agenda, or a refusal to communicate with officials of too modest rank. Neither of the three things happened; there was an exchange of friendly and courteous speeches, and Mr. Kobayashi, visibly pleased with the ceremonial of full military honours on the quay, without hesitation agreed to the proposed programme of visits, counter-visits, and audiences, and was driven in state to his hotel. In the afternoon, however, the weather broke; only then had he been informed by his Government about the current dispute on procedure.

An audience with the Governor-General and a slight alteration in the sequence of ceremonies solved the difficulty for the first few days; on the 16th the Japanese Government gave in and the negotiations could begin. It should be borne in mind that just at this time the battle of Britain was raging; that on 22nd September Vichy accepted the military occupation of Tongking by the Japanese; and that on 26th September the Tripartite Pact was concluded between Germany, Italy, and Japan.

In his conversation with the Governor-General, Jonkheer Tjarda van Starkenborgh Stachouwer, Mr. Kobayashi had stressed the necessity of closer co-operation between the Netherlands Indies and Japan, which he regarded as an inevitable consequence of the changed circumstances, but his political soundings did not touch bottom and he was deftly but firmly led back to the economic field. The first meeting *in pleno* of both delegations revealed that the Japanese had as yet little to propose for practical discussion. The only point raised was their need of mineral oil and their desire to obtain oil concessions in the Indies. But although the intended purchases of oil were called " a matter of life and death," it seemed impossible even to specify the quantities and qualities required. Meanwhile the numerous assistants had started working and studying ; whether those studies were exclusively related to economic subjects was not quite clear.

It soon transpired that a fundamental difference of opinion with regard to the character of the negotiations would make the achievement of results very difficult. Although this fact was never quite openly discussed, the lack of preparation with regard to specific points for negotiation and reliable information from various sources seemed to show that the leading idea behind the mission of Mr. Kobayashi had been more or less as follows. The quite exceptional appointment of an active cabinet minister as chief delegate, combined with the friendly attitude of the mission and the " forlorn " condition of the Netherlands Indies should have led to a general recognition of the need of close economic—and political— co-operation with Japan. As Mr. Kobayashi expressed it, the Netherlands Indies, having been closely co-operating with the United Kingdom and the United States in the past, should now " shake hands firmly " with Japan. He expected that such an attitude would, under the benevolent protection of Japan, provide security for the future of the Netherlands Indies and, incidentally, for the Netherlands. After agreement on these lines the delegation could have settled down to work out the economic profits at leisure ; hardly anything could have been denied them after that.

With regard to the meaning of the Tripartite Pact the Japanese delegation declared that its main purpose was the prevention of war in the Pacific. In this respect also, collaboration between Japan and the Netherlands Indies—and a possible agreement with the United States—might have the most happy results and promote the chances of a negotiated peace in Europe.   When pressed for an answer to the question, whether the wording of the Pact implied that Japan, claiming a leading position in East Asia, included the Netherlands Indies within that sphere, the claim was denied in a not very convincing manner.

A general meeting of both delegations at a mountain resort more or less clarified the situation, although there were rather violent discussions about the contention on the Japanese side that the Netherland delegation, in the matter of oil purchases, was acting on instructions from Washington. When this accusation was withdrawn peace was restored and eventually the following joint *communiqué* was issued, in which the ominous terms " co-existence and co-prosperity " retained a doubtful meaning.

Joint statement of the two delegations, dated 16th October 1940.

The Japanese and Netherland's delegations came together at Selabintanah near Soekaboemi from 14th till 16th October 1940 under the chairmanship of their Excellencies Ministers Kobayashi and Van Mook.

During several meetings and personal talks the general relations between Japan and the Netherlands Indies were discussed. In these discussions due attention was given to the effect of the recent pact between Japan, Germany and Italy on the relations with the Netherlands Indies. The Japanese delegation in this respect officially expressed their opinion as follows :

" In spite of the tripartite treaty recently concluded among Japan, Germany and Italy, the strong desire of Japan for the maintenance and promotion of the friendly relations between Japan and the Netherlands Indies is not affected in the least. All what is wished for by Japan is co-existence and co-prosperity with neighbouring countries." The Netherlands Delegation could appreciate this point of view.

Amongst the other points which came into discussion the most prominent item was the oil-problem. Elaborate explanations of the oil-situation in the Netherlands Indies were given by the Netherland's delegation and the chief of the Netherland's Indian Mining Bureau who was also present.

The delegations are to continue the negotiations in Batavia on the understanding that the complete scope of subjects will come into discussion in the near future.

The delegations were pleased that the negotiations were conducted in the most friendly atmosphere.

The Netherland delegation took the position that, although Japan's accession to the Tripartite Pact could not but raise serious misgivings in a country at war with Germany, they were prepared to continue negotiations on the understanding that Japan had no hostile intentions towards and did not claim leadership over the Netherlands Indies. They kept urging the submission by the Japanese of a full statement of the points to be discussed, but saw no objection to treating the matter of oil purchases separately. These purchases were mainly a matter of agreement between the Japanese buyers and the oil-producing companies, and as both parties were represented in Batavia, the contact—for which the Netherland delegation would be pleased to lend their good offices—would be easy.

In the meantime the Japanese demands with regard to the purchase of mineral oil and oil products had gradually become more defined. About a week after the opening conference the following specification was produced, enumerating Japan's annual minimum requirements—over and above the regular sales made by the companies and allowed by the Japanese Government—of Netherlands Indies' oil in tons of 2,240 lb.

A. Crude oil :		
1. Aviation crude . . .	1,100,000	tons
2. Crude oil for lubricants .	100,000	,,
3. Other	1,050,000	,,
B. Aviation spirit (over 87 octane) .	400,000	,,
C. Diesel oil . . .	500,000	,,
Total . .	3,150,000	tons

It was, in part erroneously, contended that contracts had already been agreed upon for the delivery of 120,000 tons of aviation crude, 792,000 tons of other crudes, and 100,000 tons of aviation spirit to be delivered per annum. A five years' guarantee of the Netherlands Indies Government was demanded that these minimum requirements should be regularly fulfilled.

Although these demands were preposterous, the matter lay for the moment in the hands of the representatives of the oil companies. There could be no question of a guarantee; the part of the Netherlands Indies Government in the deal was only supervisory.

The Netherlands and the Netherlands Indies had to make the prosecution of the war their paramount concern, and could not deviate from their proven policy of non-discrimination and non-preference towards all countries with which friendly relations existed. On these grounds the supervision of oil sales had to be concerned, mainly, with two points : reservation of the products most essential for war for our own use and that of our Allies, and non-interference with the regular sales to third parties. With regard to the internal position the Netherlands Indies Government had to object to any substantial increase of oil production, as the known reserves were already on the low side. With these provisions in mind the Netherland delegation could not but point out that an increase of sales to Japan from the present level of about 600,000 tons a year to about 3,750,000 tons a year was completely impossible.

With regard to the matter of oil concessions the delegation had no objection to providing general information from published sources, but they could not see their way to open negotiations on that point as long as a full agenda had not been submitted. The following letters and memoranda exchanged on this point supply the necessary illustration. The request for a Government guarantee was subsequently dropped by the Japanese.

Letter addressed to the Chairman of the Netherland delegation by Mr. T. Mukai on 24th
September 1940.

Re : Study on petroleum-oil.

With reference to our oil-business with your country, I would
like to know from Your Excellency several points on which our
knowledge is insufficient.

The main points of my enquiries are as described in the sheet
attached hereto.

In this connection, I shall be much obliged to you, if Your
Excellency would be so kind to give me and my party informations
as minutely as possible and provide us with useful pieces of
reference, and furthermore, to afford us opportunities for actual
study of oil-producing districts and refineries, and to introduce
me and my party to the concerned.

As I think it convenient for me and my party to take up lodgings
in Bandoeng on principal in order to be favoured with your
esteemed informations and worthy advices promptly, I take the
liberty to beg you for your another favour to inform our purposes
to the Head of the Mine Department and other authorities in
Bandoeng and let them give us help in regard to points as stated
in attached sheet.

I shall appreciate highly your esteemed assistances and express
in advance my most profound thanks to Your Excellency and
other authorities for kind informations and facilities to be given
to us.

The attached sheet was very succinct :

POINTS OF STUDY

1. Products of petroleum-oil in Netherlands East Indies and
   its qualities ;
2. Equipments for oil-refinings and its capacities ;
3. Loading and shipping facilities and its capacities per port ;
4. Present situations and conditions of all concessions under
   exploitation ;
5. Present situations and conditions of mining-area reserved
   by the Government.

Note addressed to Mr. T. Mukai by the Netherland
delegation on 7th October 1940.

With reference to the letter of September 24th, addressed by
Mr. Mukai to the Chairman of the Netherlands Delegation for

the economic conference at Batavia, the Netherlands Delegation has the honour to present to the Japanese Delegation a memorandum containing a general survey of the oil-situation in the Netherlands Indies.

To the memorandum is added a number of annexes regarding the present situation of mining concessions and contracts, the reservations and closures of territories by the Government and the models of 5a-exploration and exploitation contracts.

The Chief of the Mining Bureau and his experts are prepared to add further information as far as wanted at the headquarters of the Netherlands Delegation, Koningsplein West 2, Batavia.

In the letter of Mr. Mukai the wish was expressed that the Government should afford him and his party opportunities for actual study of oil-producing districts and refineries and should introduce them to the companies concerned. As far as regards the last-mentioned request the necessary introductions will gladly be given, but it must be understood that visits to the refineries and the oilfields can only be granted by the respective owners and that the Government, although its officers are free to inspect all the mining enterprises in the Netherlands Indies, has no power to grant such a right to third parties.

MEMORANDUM

I. PRODUCTION OF CRUDE OIL AND OIL PRODUCTS IN THE NETHERLANDS INDIES.

The production of crude oil for the years 1937, 1938 and 1939 in the several oil-producing districts of the Netherlands Indies is tabulated here below:

Production of crude oil in metric tons

Territory	1939	1938	1937
Java and Madoera . .	840,950	933,595	960,125
Palembang . . .	3,125,035	2,747,023	2,784,448
Djambi . . .	1,211,270	1,010,713	885,832
East coast of Sumatra .	162,130	198,158	189,226
Atjeh and Dependencies .	821,885	706,942	630,631
East Borneo . . .	996,691	985,055	1,005,781
Tarakan . . .	683,686	735,098	733,619
Bunju	—	—	207
Moluccas . . .	107,047	81,560	72,139
Total . . .	7,948,694	7,398,144	7,262,008

Out of these amounts of crude the refining industry produced the following quantities and specifications of oil products :

Oil products in metric tons

Oil Products	1939	1938	1937
Gasoline . . .	2,099,828	1,850,927	1,837,283
Aviation gasoline under 87 octane . .	416,031	401,381	308,633
White spirit . .	51,756	58,211	75,041
Kerosine . . .	1,037,242	931,248	1,090,102
Residue . . .	1,495,406	1,626,822	1,609,817
Solar and Diesel oil .	1,406,986	1,165,926	1,096,754
Lubricating oil . .	29,242	25,138	32,527
Impregnating oil . .	19,306	17,197	8,140
Paraffine, wax and ceresine	91,994	78,028	83,266
Asphalt, asphalt oil, etc.	29,288	24,683	21,252
Coke . . .	20,066	7,152	9,345
Destillation gas . .	394,097	178,330	158,473
Losses . . .	154,873	255,256	171,465
Total . .	7,246,115	6,620,299	6,502,098

The product specified as gasoline is ordinary motor gasoline of 72 octane or less, and the product specified as aviation gasoline is normal gasoline of 87 octane or less, made by treating normal gasoline with tetra-aethyl lead. High octane aviation gasoline was not produced in the Netherlands Indian refineries before April of this year, when two plants at Pladjoe and Soengei Gerong came into production ; these plants have a yearly productive capacity of about 200,000 metric tons of high octane aviation gasoline (over 87 octane).

The crude oil production shows an extensive range of qualities and specifications, necessitating in many cases specially adapted refining outfits in order to get the best possible economic results. Of the several crudes probably only the Brandan crude of North Sumatra, with a production of between 750,000 and 900,000 tons a year, might be considered as an aviation crude, though of course some of the other light crudes would yield small amounts of higher octane gasolines by destillation. The Brandan fields are at their maximum production and have a calculated reserve of not more than 6 years at the present level. Their output is largely indispensable for the alimentation of the Brandan refinery.

Among the several Netherlands Indian crudes there is no raw material available for the extraction of a satisfactory lubricating oil; up to the present only about 30,000 tons of lubricating oil of a second grade quality are produced in the Netherlands Indies.

II.   REFINING PLANTS.

The Netherlands Indian oil industry does not as a rule sell crude oil; all crude oil, with few exceptions, is refined in the Netherlands Indies. This system is economically sound, as it causes less waste of raw material, reduces transport expenses, enables the companies to distribute their products directly to the neighbouring natural markets and facilitates concentration in large and economically located plants. To change this system would mean a serious loss of income for the Netherlands Indies and a decrease of labour and would mean an appreciable loss of efficiency in production. Furthermore, it must be well understood that a refining plant, built at great capital expense, can only be a profitable enterprise as long as it is worked at or near its total capacity. As the Government has a fiscal interest in the financial results of the oil companies, this matter is of equal concern to the companies as to the Government.

The several refining plants are adapted to the kind of crude which is produced in their neighbourhood and which they use as raw material.

In Balikpapan crude oil with a paraffine basis is refined by destillation in trumbles and further refined for the production of gasoline and kerosine by the Edeleanu process. Part of the gasoline is cracked in Dubbs plants. The residue is made into paraffine and for a small part into second grade lubricating oil.

The refinery at Pladjoe uses crude oils with both asphalt and paraffine basis in trumble-plants, cracking-plants, an Edeleanu-factory and reforming-plants for producing normal motor gasoline. A new plant has been built for manufacturing high octane aviation gasoline by polymerization and hydrogenation. Besides there is a paraffine factory and a small factory for lubricating oil.

The refinery at Soengei Gerong uses a heavy oil with a high percentage of paraffine for destillation in continual-stills and trumble-plants for the production of heavy gasoline, kerosine and residue. All these products are cracked, as is the paraffine obtained from the residue. The final products are normal motor gasoline, kerosine, Diesel oil and coke. Part of the normal gasoline is made into high octane aviation gasoline by the alkylation process in a newly erected plant. The refinery also includes a large paraffine factory.

The refinery at Pangkalan-Brandan uses crude oil with an asphalt-basis to produce normal gasoline and kerosine by destillation and refining. A small part of these products is cracked to obtain a better quality of normal gasoline.

The refinery at Tjepoe uses the same kinds of crude as Balikpapan and refines them in the same way.

The total capacity of the seven refining plants—including two very small plants at Wonokromo and Kapoean—is round about 8,000,000 metric tons a year; the actual throughput in 1939 was 7,246,000 metric tons.

III. LOADING AND SHIPPING FACILITIES.

The information about loading and shipping facilities shall be produced as soon as it can be made clear for which ports the data are wanted with regard to the prospective exports to Japan.

IV. GENERAL SITUATION OF THE OIL PRODUCTION.

The most prominent characteristic of the present situation as to the production of crude oil in the Netherlands Indies is the gradual deterioration of the ratio between reserves and production. The production of crude oil reached an all-time high in 1939 at 7,948,860 metric tons, whereas the calculated reserves reached an all-time low of 6·8 years of possible production at the present level.

When this calculation was made in 1935 the ratio still stood at 8·3 years, but in 1938 it had already fallen to 6·9 years.

This development clearly indicates that the increase of production has been out of proportion with the increase of reserves. In other oil-producing countries the normal ratio is between 10 and 20 years.

In this situation any considerable increase of production would mean that a sharp decrease would inevitably follow in the near future, unless the continued exploration should give much better results than it has done during the last years.

In 1939 the oil companies, working in the Netherlands Indies, exploited 43 concessions allotted before 1924, which have been in exploitation for a long time. The production of these concessions is diminishing and the number of non-profitable areas increases. In 1939 30 of these concessions were worked at a profit and 13 at a financial loss.

After 1924 the old-style concession was abolished and the new 5a-exploration contract was established. On these contracts the oil companies have continued their extensive and costly explorations, but the results of these explorations have been much less satisfying than those of the old concessions.

In 1939 30 areas under 5a-contract were in exploitation, of which only 5 showed a financial profit, whereas the accounts of the other 25 fields showed a deficit. The expensive and difficult character of exploration in the Netherlands Indies is illustrated by the fact that these deficits at the end of that year had already mounted up to f 80,000,000, which figure does not include the exploration costs of the areas recently allotted. The present level of exploration costs amounts to an average of f 17,000,000 a year, the expenses on this head in 1939 having been f 22½ million.

Another analysis shows that the areas opened in the successive periods since the beginning of the Netherlands Indian oil industry have a tendency of being less and less remunerative. In the concessions before 1924 1·3 % of the total area of 673,146 ha has become productive. For the 5a-contracts issued between 1924 and 1930 the figures are : total area 573,180 ha, productive area 0·5 %. In 1931 5a-contracts were issued for 687,410 ha, which have only yielded a productive area of 0·35 % ; for the period between 1933 and 1936 these figures are 11,471,111 ha and 0·002 %, whereas the contracts issued between 1937 and 1939 for a total area of 3,247,710 ha have not yet shown any results at all.

All the foregoing figures have been computed by the Government Mining Bureau after extensive and scrupulous investigations both of the accounts of the companies and on the field.

It will be clear from these data that only a complete change for the better in the exploration results would justify a considerable increase of the yearly production and that as long as such a change does not happen, such an increase would be detrimental to the interests of the oil-industry, the buyers and prospective buyers of the Netherlands Indian oil and the Netherlands Indies as a whole. The consensus of opinion at present is that the oil production, as compared with the reserve position, is dangerously high already.

V. Outline of the Policy Concerning Oil Concessions in the Netherlands Indies.

On account of the economic importance of oil, in 1919 the Mining-law was changed in order to lift out this mineral from the normal list of minerals mentioned in that law.

No new concessions for oil were obtainable in the general way provided by that law, so that the Government obtained complete discretionary powers for the disposal of exploration and exploitation contracts for oil.

After that an independent oil policy developed, which resulted in the conclusion of a number of 5a-exploitation contracts with the B.P.M. and N.K.P.M., oil companies which had been working in this country since 1890 and 1912.

In 1921 a joint company was established, in which the Government and the B.P.M. participated, under the name of Nederlandsch Indische Aardolie Maatschappij (N.I.A.M.) which has its principal sphere of activity in Djambi. The exploitation of its fields and the sales of its products are contractually assigned to the B.P.M.

In 1934, just before the general examination of the oil reserves in the Netherlands Indies was undertaken, the Pacific Oil Company was admitted in Central Sumatra.

As the results of the investigation concerning oil reserves were very disappointing, the Government decided in principle not to admit any more oil companies into the oil industry. As a result of this decision a request of the Algemeene Exploratie Mij. to conclude a 5a-contract was refused.

In accordance with this decision the remaining prospective oil-areas not under concession or contract are divided into spheres of interest, destined for the alimentation of the several large and expensive refineries of the B.P.M. and N.K.P.M., whereas the Pacific Oil Company has been allotted an area in Central Sumatra as a sphere of interest.

A large part of New Guinea, where exploration was started four years ago, was allotted under a 5a-contract to a joint company formed by the B.P.M., the N.K.P.M. and the Pacific under the name of Nederlandsch Nieuw Guinea Petroleum Maatschappij (N.N.G.P.M.) in 1936.

As the results of further explorations continued to be poor, large areas were added to the contractual field of action of the companies, with the result that their spheres of interest now cover the greater part of the territories where oil-deposits are geologically possible.

Only a few separate areas have not yet acquired a positive destination.

Of these may be mentioned the territory around Sangkoelirang (Mangkaliat), where the Japanese Borneo Oil Company possesses the concessions " Kari Orang," " Koetei I " and " Koetei II "; a limited area in Celebes, opposite the island Peleng (Manado), and the North-Eastern and South-Eastern parts of Netherlands New Guinea.

These areas might come under consideration for extension of Japanese oil-interests ; especially so as regards the Mangkaliat peninsula, where the Japanese already hold a concession and where several extensive blocks, offering reasonable chances of success, might be allotted under a 5a-contract.

As regards the legal position it should be understood that the right of prospecting for oil can only be obtained by a 5a-exploration contract, which implies a preference to an exploitation contract if oil is found in sufficient quantities. The general prospecting rights under the Mining-law are only used for general geological examination ; a 5a-exploration contract must be concluded to explore for oil.

Prospecting permits are granted to the now operating oil companies only in those areas, which may be considered to lie within the sphere of interest of the company concerned.

Finally, it should be mentioned that it is a fixed policy of the Government to provide neutral zones around and between the 5a-contract areas to obviate the subdivision of oilpools.

After a few more difficulties and hesitations, direct contact was established between Mr. Mukai, who had been put in charge of the oil business by the Japanese, and the companies. There were many rumours, at the time, about this matter ; the clearest statement of facts is contained in the proposals as formulated by the companies and transmitted to Mr. Mukai on 8th October. There was no change in the figures afterwards ; the proposals were accepted on the 18th of October, and the contracts were eventually drawn up on this basis. Compared with the original demands the net results for Japan were the acquisition of :

(a) 120,000 tons of aviation crude instead of 1,100,000 tons ;

(b) 100,000 tons of crude for lubricants of an extremely doubtful quality ; but eventually to be used as Diesel oil ;

(c) 540,000 tons of other crudes instead of 1,050,000 tons ;

(d) a single spot sale of 33,000 tons aviation spirit instead of 400,000 tons annually ;

(e) 116,500 tons of Diesel oil instead of 500,000 tons.

The complete and reasoned offer of the oil companies is given *in extenso* here below :

Letter addressed to Mr. T. Mukai by the Chairman of the Netherland delegation on 8th October 1940.

The President of the Netherlands Delegation for the Economic Negotiations with Japan has transmitted to the oil companies a list showing the quantities of petroleum and products desired by Japan from the Netherlands Indies, and has requested the companies to give their most sympathetic and best consideration to the subject.

The companies have been pleased to comply with the President's request and to furnish you herewith their views and proposals with respect to said requirements.

MEMORANDUM

The oil companies have given serious consideration to the requirements as listed in the statement presented to the Netherlands Delegation for the Economic Negotiations with Japan on September 25, 1940, with the view of making the largest possible quantities available. In view of the following circumstances the companies are unable to make available the full quantities as listed, but they are prepared to make offers in addition to the quantities already arranged in Japan, all of which quantities are listed later on in this memorandum.

1. The oil companies have developed markets for their Netherlands Indies production of petroleum products by building up distribution and sales organisations in the Netherlands Indies and neighbouring countries, including Japan. During this development shipments of the companies from the Netherlands Indies have steadily increased to all of these countries except Japan, to which country, on the contrary, the shipments of petroleum products from the Netherlands Indies have declined from 927,000 tons in 1937 to 547,000 tons in 1939.

2. Most of these countries therefore have become dependent upon the Netherlands Indies for their principal supplies of petroleum products and the companies have incurred an obligation to keep those countries adequately and efficiently supplied. It would be unfair to those countries and unsound economically to consider replacing shipments from the Netherlands Indies by shipments from

other more distant sources of supply in order to provide for increased shipments to Japan.

3. Increased shipments to Japan can only be made to a limited extent by increasing the production of oil in the Netherlands Indies, as the calculated oil reserves in this country are so limited that according to the data now available a substantial increase in production of crude oil would not only greatly reduce the ultimate total recovery of oil (by producing inefficiently at a high rate) but would lead to the depletion of existing reserves within a few years. This would not only be very detrimental to the interests of the Netherlands Indies as a whole, but would render useless the extensive refinery facilities which the companies have provided at a very large capital investment and on the basis that adequate crude supplies for these refineries would be available for a considerable number of years.

The object of the oil companies is not only the production of crude oil but also the manufacture, distribution and sale of finished petroleum products. To accomplish their overall objective the companies have erected large refineries in the vicinity of the oil fields with a total capacity equalling approximately the total amount of crude oil which can be efficiently produced. Therefore it is extremely difficult to make any crude oil available for sale as such.

According to the information received by the oil companies from Japan, incorrect quantities are listed in the statement of September 25th as having been agreed in Tokyo. The companies understand that discussions covered a monthly quantity of 76,000 tons of crude oil for one year. This 76,000 tons included 16,000 tons to be supplied from outside the Netherlands Indies (i.e. Miri, British North Borneo). Of the 60,000 tons per month from the Netherlands Indies discussed in Tokyo, the companies understood that only 40,000 tons have actually been sold with a commitment of one year delivery.

The statement further lists 100,000 tons of aviation gasoline as having been agreed in Tokyo. The companies here have no knowledge of any such commitment. They are advised that definite sales were made of three cargoes of high octane aviation gasoline totalling 33,000 tons and 8,400 tons per month of 70 octane motor gasoline. This quantity of 70 octane motor gasoline is at the rate of 100,000 tons per annum, but the companies understand that no commitment was made for a period of one year. They are, however, prepared to accept it as a definite commitment for six months.

The quantities which the companies can make available are as follows :

BATAAFSCHE PETROLEUM MAATSCHAPPIJ

Period Sales

Product.	Quantities already settled in Japan. Annual Rate.	Additional quantities which are available. Annual Rate.	Total. Annual Rate.
1. Aviation Crude (Light Brandan Crude)	120,000	nil	120,000
2. Special Tarakan Crude [1]	nil	100,000	100,000
3. Other Grades of Crude	230,000	130,000	360,000
4. Aviation Gasoline	nil	nil	nil
5. 69/70 Oct. Straight Run Gasoline [2]	nil	50,000	50,000
6. 70 Oct. Motor Gasoline	100,000	nil	100,000
7. 63 Oct. Motor Gasoline [2]	nil	25,000	25,000
8. Gas Oil [2]	nil	50,000	50,000
9. Diesel Oil [2]	nil	50,000	50,000
10. Tarakan Diesel Oil Mixture [1]	nil	66,500	66,500
11. Fuel Oil [2]	nil	73,000	73,000
	450,000	544,500	994,500

[1] Special Tarakan crude is of a quality from which lubricating oils could be manufactured. It is so used in the Balikpapan refinery. If not required for this purpose it can be used as a Diesel oil and could be offered in addition to 10.

[2] These products are offered *in toto*. They are the products obtained from increased production and must be either taken as a whole or not at all. Delivery could only commence after three months.

Spot Sales

Product.	Quantities already settled in Japan.	Additional quantities which are available.	Total.
	Annual Rate.	Annual Rate.	Annual Rate.
Aviation Gasoline	33,000	nil	33,000
Diesel Oil	16,000	nil	16,000
	49,000	nil	49,000

No further spot sales can be offered now.

In addition the Bataafsche proposed to supply Japan during the next year, under Rising Sun Petroleum Co. sales or import quotas, 376,000 tons of finished products. The total quantities which have been made and are hereby made available to Japan are *at the rate* of 1,370,500 tons per annum under period sales and 49,000 tons under spot sales, as follows :

Under Period Contracts

(1) Crude Oil	.	.	.	580,000 tons
(2) Products	.	.	.	414,500 tons
(3) Import or Sales Quotas	.	.	376,000 tons

1,370,500 tons

Under Spot Sales

(1) Aviation Gasoline	.	.	.	33,000 tons
(2) Diesel Oil	.	.	.	16,000 tons

1,419,500 tons

The additional quantities of crude oil and products can be offered *at the rate* of 544,500 tons per annum on the basis of contracts for a normal period not exceeding six months, with the understanding that delivery of the products mentioned on the preceding page under 5, 7, 8, 9 and 11 can only be made after three months. Contracts for deliveries for a subsequent period may be negotiated to the expiration of the initial contracts. (See Note.)

NEDERLANDSCHE KOLONIALE PETROLEUM MAATSCHAPPIJ

Product.	Quantities already settled in Japan. Annual Rate.	Additional quantities which are available. Annual Rate.	Total. Annual Rate.
1. Aviation Crude Oil	nil	nil	nil
2. Lubricating Crude Oil	nil	nil	nil
3. Other Grades of Crude Oil	130,000	50,000	180,000
4. Aviation Gasoline	nil	nil	nil
5. Diesel Oil	nil	nil	nil
6. Motor Gasoline	nil	75,000	75,000
7. Kerosene	nil	57,000	57,000
	130,000	182,000	312,000

All quantities in tons and at the annual rate indicated.

In addition please note that N.K.P.M. propose to supply to Japan during the next year, under S.V.O.C. sales quotas, 118,000 tons of finished products. The total quantities which can be made available to Japan are therefore at the rate of 430,000 tons per annum, as follows:

(1) Crude Oil	.	.	.	180,000 tons
(2) Gasoline	.	.	.	75,000 tons
(3) Kerosene	.	.	.	57,000 tons
				312,000 tons
For Sales Quotas		.	.	118,000 tons
				430,000 tons

The additional quantities of crude oil and products can be offered at the rate of 182,000 tons per annum on the basis of contracts for normal periods not exceeding six months. Contracts for deliveries for a subsequent period may be negotiated prior to the expiration of the initial contracts. If actual purchase is desired it will be possible to agree in Batavia on the quantities, basic price formula, and terms and method of payment, but actual contracts must be signed in Japan with the Standard Vacuum Oil Company.

A summary of the above quantities is as follows :

B.P.M.	.	.	.	1,419,500 tons
N.K.P.M.	.	.	.	430,000 tons

1,849,500 tons

NOTE.—Such contracts should be concluded in Japan with the Rising Sun. If, however, desired, price formula and payment could be negotiated and agreed upon here.

Suddenly, two days after the acceptance of these proposals, Mr. Kobayashi announced his recall on the 20th of October, and left on the 22nd. The reason given was alternately that he could no longer be spared in his department, and that he had to be home for the 2,600th anniversary of the creation of the Japanese Empire by the Sun Goddess. The real reason was, of course, that the intended general agreement to collaborate had not materialized and that the conclusion of the oil contracts offered a welcome opportunity to call it a day. The Japanese Government announced that Messrs. Ota and Saito would continue the negotiations. The farewell communication from the Japanese delegation in their original composition gave the following appreciation of what had been achieved :

Note handed to the Netherland delegation by the Japanese delegation on 21st October 1940.

The Japanese delegation has the honour to express their great appreciation for an elaborate explanation of petroleum situation contained in the Note of October 7th of the Netherlands delegation. The Japanese delegation wishes to call the attention of the Netherlands delegation to the fact that after negotiations between Mr. Mukai and two petroleum companies, the proposals of these companies concerning oil supply to Japan have shown a very wide difference in quantity as well as in quality from those of Mr. Mukai and it is to be emphasized that the proposed quantity of supply of aviation gasoline and aviation crude to Japan to which Japan attaches a great importance, is as good as nil.

The Netherlands delegation, however, is well aware of the Japanese interest in petroleum problems and the Japanese delegation would be much obliged, if the Netherlands delegation are good enough to do their utmost, in the spirit of mutual welfare to comply with the Japanese proposals by any means like shifting of trade route, etc.

The Japanese delegation have the pleasure to add that Japan has also a very big interest in exploitation of oil wells and that the Netherlands policies on allocating spheres of interests for existing companies are hardly satisfactory for Japan.

The Japanese delegation are very much desirous to acquire rights of access to the territories now in exploration or exploitation as well as to the Government reserves.

Mr. Mukai, however, is ready to enter at once into negotiations with authorities concerned about the Government reserve areas in the above-mentioned Note of the Netherlands delegation.

As far as time permitted the farewell ceremonies were as elaborate as the first reception, but they were less cheerful. Mr. Kobayashi, a typically Japanese businessman who had been very successful in combining the exploitation of an electric railway and a popular burlesque theatre in Japan, but who had little knowledge of the world at large and no familiarity at all with the Netherlands Indies, clearly felt that his mission had failed. His tough co-delegates, of whom Mr. Saito was preparing to leave, as he had already been relieved of his post and replaced by Mr. Y. Ishizawa—reappointed Consul-General on the 15th of October [1]—had nothing to propose and could only reiterate that they were expecting instructions from Tokyo any time. The continuously changing swarm of assistants remained in force and collected information where they could—not of a purely economic nature.

Only Mr. Mukai made an effort to continue the negotiations by entering two requests concerning oil concessions. They were almost insolently exacting and read as follows :

Letters addressed to the Chairman of the Netherland delegation by Mr. T. Mukai on 29th October 1940.

I. Re OIL TERRITORIES

With reference to your memorandum dated the 7th inst. (item No. 5), and the subsequent conversation exchanged during the

[1] He arrived in Batavia on 27th November.

interview between delegates of the Netherland Indies and Japan, I am given to understand that the undermentioned districts and areas, which you have not yet committed to any other party or parties, will be considered as an interest for Japan :   .

Borneo—the districts of Kaliorang and Koetai about		1,300,000 ha.
Celebes—the district opposite to the Pelang Island	about	163,000 ,,
Dutch New Guinea :		
North-eastern shoreland . . .	about	1,200,000 ,,
Middle-eastern interior . . .	about	3,500,000 ,,
South-eastern shoreland . . .	about	9,000,000 ,,
Aroe Archipelago, south-east to Dutch New Guinea	about	850,000 ,,
Schouten Archipelago, north-east to Dutch New Guinea	about	350,000 ,,
Total	about	16,363,000 ha.

As Japan is desirous to carry on explorations and exploitations in future in the entire dimensions of the above districts upon completion of the general geological examinations, I shall be obliged by your acknowledgment of the whole of these districts as Japan's sphere of interest, and the necessary steps according to your Mining Law will be taken in due course in accordance with your suggestions.

Furthermore, in view of the rapid increase in the demand of Petroleum in Japan, I would like to express the strong desire of Japan that the following areas will be assigned to the Japanese interests in addition to the above-mentioned areas :

(1) Borneo :		
An area, opposite to the Tarakan Island, northward from the Bengara River to the boundaries of British North Borneo . .	about	400,000 ha.
(2) Sumatra :		
An area extending south-eastwards from Medan and along the River Asahan	about	700,000 ,,
Total	about	1,100,000 ha.

Your kind considerations to this matter will be much appreciated, and I am quite certain that your acceptance will serve greatly
in promoting the closer relationship between Netherlands Indies
and Japan.

I also beg to mention that Japan may consider the capital
participation of Netherlands Indies in these enterprises.

II. *Re* PARTICIPATION OF JAPANESE CAPITAL

While the transaction on Petroleum between Netherland
Indies and Japan are in a trend of a steady increase in the future,
it is needless to say that Japanese oil circles are focussing their
interests on the petroleum of the Netherland Indies, and consequently they are having an earnest desire to directly exploit the
petroleum resources.

You have fully appreciated these circumstances and are direct-
ing us to achieve Japan's aim with your special attention, for which
I express herein my thanks.

However, with an eye to the furtherance of the prosperity and
friendship of both countries, I beg to mention that it is strongly
desired on the side of Japan to participate in the capital of the
N.V. Nederlandsche Indische Aardolie Maatschappij.

As I understand that your Government hold a considerable
amount of shares in the aforesaid undertakings, I hope that your
Excellency would consider the allotment of part of these shares
to Japan.

In case this proposal of ours be favoured with your approval,
I would greatly appreciate your informing me of your terms and
conditions.

Poor Mr. Mukai, who was a conscientious businessman
of gentle disposition, did not relish his diplomatic duties at
all.   He disliked them more than ever when his requests were
met by a reminder that the Netherland delegation refused to
proceed in a piecemeal fashion and preferred to wait until
a complete agenda would be agreed upon.   He felt im-
mensely relieved when he was allowed to return to Japan a
few weeks afterwards.   His successor, Mr. Y. Ito, Managing
Director of Mitsui Bussan Kaisha, arrived before the end of
the year, but he had to wait, too, until the reconstructed
Japanese delegation were ready with their programme.   He
did so with no very good grace.

In the meantime the Netherland Minister had handed an *aide mémoire*, on the 15th of November, to Mr. Ohashi, Vice-Minister of Foreign Affairs in Tokyo, to draw the attention of the Japanese Government to the fact that the negotiations were at a standstill for lack of subject-matter, and to recommend their discontinuation. This was answered by a *note verbale* on 20th November, announcing the imminent appointment of a new special envoy who was to instil renewed activity into the proceedings. On 28th November this successor turned out to be Mr. K. Yoshizawa, Member of the House of Peers and former Minister of Foreign Affairs. He was due to arrive in Batavia on the 23rd of December and would carry on with the aid of Mr. Ishizawa, the new Consul-General. Mr. Ota, the remaining member of the former trio, faded out of the picture, and disappeared in February, unwept, unhonoured, and unsung.

This interval of more than two months, although quiet in some respects, presented a number of very annoying and disturbing features. The general public, both in the Netherlands Indies and elsewhere, could hardly believe that nothing happened. The personnel of the Japanese delegation and of the Consulate General were as busy as bees, and Japanese propaganda was making the most of the oil deal and threatening the haughty and insincere Netherlands Indies with fearful things to come. Wild rumours became current and obtained a wide publicity ; they even had their echo in the House of Commons. It was almost impossible to rectify them without committing indiscretions ; the conventions of diplomatic intercourse were still scrupulously observed. And all the while the Japanese preparations for the coming military campaign in the Nanyo (the South Sea regions) were pushed on with diligence and elaborate accuracy. Stacks of information left Batavia for Tokyo by the ever more frequent couriers, and although it is rather improbable that the spying crowd of " experts " got hold of real secrets, they certainly amassed and sifted all the available data necessary for the landing expeditions that were to come. The Japanese, who had made it a serious crime for foreigners in their country even to copy published trade statistics, must have regarded all this ant-like activity as a great achievement in military intelligence. They certainly considered us to be fools because we gave them access to our public records. Perhaps we were.

Only one event, happening more or less back-stage at this time, seemed slightly to ease the situation. There had been a growing agitation in Japan for the use of the yen as the chief medium of exchange in the " Co-prosperity Sphere " and against the dominating position of the dollar. There was more behind this movement than mere propaganda ; the Japanese feared that their not inconsiderable dollar balances in the United States might be frozen at any moment. To further their designs in this respect the chief representative of the Yokohama Specie Bank in the Indies, Mr. Y. Imagawa, acting for the Japanese exchange control, approached the Japanese and Netherland delegations with a project to establish a free and unlimited exchangeability between the yen and the Netherlands Indies guilder at fixed and agreed rates, instead of the customary mutual payments in dollars. The proposal was referred to direct discussion between the Yokohama Specie Bank and De Javasche Bank (the bank of issue in the Netherlands Indies) and reduced to an arrangement for direct payment in yen and guilders as long as credit balances stayed within certain narrow limits ; any excess balances, however, were to remain collectable in dollars as before. The agreement, which was perfected a few days before the arrival of Mr. Yoshizawa, was hailed as a major economic victory by the Japanese and as a favourable omen for the renewal of general negotiations. The practical advantages, from a Japanese point of view, were negligible, as the oil deliveries had been contracted for in dollars and the remaining trade continued to show a negative balance for the Indies.

At last, on the 28th of December 1940, the inevitable *Nissho Maru* edged alongside again in Priok harbour and Mr. Yoshizawa set foot on Netherlands Indies soil.

CHAPTER V

THE YOSHIZAWA MISSION

THE atmosphere around the Yoshizawa mission might be less explosive than that in which the Kobayashi mission had arrived, but there was a growing tenseness. On the one hand, the limitation of exports from the United States to Japan had been extended to iron and steel scrap on 16th October, and the Burma Road had been reopened on 18th October 1940. On the other, the occupation of Northern Indo-China by Japanese troops and the gradual strengthening of Japanese influence in Thailand converted the theoretical possibility of trade in war materials with Germany, via the Siberian railway, into a very practical proposition, particularly with regard to rubber and tin. The general outlook had been brightened by the British successes in North Africa and the magnificent stand of the Greeks, but in the succeeding months the shadows of reverse and disaster in Yugoslavia, Greece, Crete, and Libya, were to darken the picture again. The blockade had to be tightened to the utmost, and all the time Herr Wohltat, head of the German economic mission to Japan, was in Japan to see to it that Germany got in as much as possible through the back door.

There was a sense of unreality in the exact repetition of the ceremonial welcome at Tandjong Priok, like the sensation one sometimes has of things having happened before in a completely identical way. There was a marked difference, however, between the new Japanese team and the old. The Japanese Government choose their representatives with an expert eye on the mood they want to convey. Mr. Kobayashi's group had been constituted to present a simple, peremptory, and essentially Japanese mask ; they had come to lay down the Imperial law by the mere weight of their august presence.

Mr. Yoshizawa and Mr. Ishizawa, on the contrary, were trained diplomats and men of the world, suave and tenacious, prepared for skilful and courteous negotiation. Studied urbanity and sometimes even wit took the place of aggressive and undiscerning stolidity. Apparently the time for armed compulsion had not yet come, and if the Netherlands Indies could not be impressed by a show of mighty condescension, Japan would resort to the art of bargaining for the nonce.

This time the Japanese proposals were not so slow in coming. New Year, which always means elaborate visits and felicitations for the Japanese, might delay the work for a few days, but on the 16th of January 1941, the Japanese delegation presented their first memorandum. Its general tenor might have been forecast from the remarks Mr. Yoshizawa made during a conversation with the Governor-General, when he stressed the necessity of closer collaboration between the two countries, and Japan's ardent desire to participate in the exploitation of the Indies. The memorandum contained a statement of general policy and a number of sweeping demands, aiming at the complete inclusion of the Netherlands Indies in the Co-prosperity Sphere. The reader may judge for himself.

Memorandum presented by the Japanese delegation
on 16th January 1941.

Most of the vast territories of the Netherlands-Indies, abundant in natural resources, are very thinly populated and still remain undeveloped, waiting for exploitation and development in wide fields. It is beyond question that the exploitation and the development of these areas would bring benefit not only to the Netherlands-Indies but also to Japan and, at the same time would contribute to the welfare of the world.

As a matter of fact, Japan and the Netherlands-Indies stand in the relation of economic interdependence, the former being geographically situated much nearer to the latter than any other European or American powers. Accordingly, a great importance should be stressed upon the necessity of strengthening the economic relations between the two countries. Japan is earnestly desirous of participating in the exploitation of the natural resources in the Netherlands-Indies, and of promoting the trade and other economic relations with her. It is Japan's firm conviction that a great contribution would also be made towards the prosperity of the Netherlands-Indies herself, if the Netherlands-Indies Government would see their way to meet Japan's desires and facilitate the economic activities in the Netherlands-Indies of Japanese nationals.

In the view above-mentioned, the Japanese Government wish to present the following proposals to the Netherlands-Indies Government :

I.   THE ENTRY OF JAPANESE NATIONALS AND OTHER AFFAIRS

(1) Modification of the restriction of entry.

    (a) Procedure laid down in the Foreign Labour Ordinance (Ordonnantie Vreemdelingenarbeid) be simplified in order to permit entry of the Japanese nationals, possessing pass-ports issued by the Japanese Government, up to the maximum number as stipulated in the Netherlands-Indies Entry Ordinance (Toelatingsbesluit)—for example, 1,633 persons in the year of 1940, with the exception of the following cases mentioned in (b) and (c).

    (b) Permission of entry be granted to Japanese nationals who are required for carrying on exploitation and development enterprises in Buiten Gewesten—especially Sumatra, Borneo and Great East, where speedy development can hardly be expected without the entry of substantial number of Japanese nationals.

    (c) Japanese nationals who are permitted to enter for temporary stay, be not included in the number, mentioned in (a) above cited.

    (d) The entry tax be abolished.

(2) Elimination of difficulties concerning explorations.

    Any difficulties whatever concerning explorations, necessary for carrying on enterprises and for other economic activities, be eliminated.

(3) Freedom of medical practice by Japanese doctors.

    Restrictions imposed upon medical practice be modified in order that Japanese nationals, who are qualified in Japan as doctors (including dentists), may be granted permission for their medical practice in the Netherlands-Indies.

(4) Promotion of rationalization of the management of Japanese enterprises.

Where Japan and the Netherlands-Indies joint-enterprises are desired as a form of management of enterprises, necessary assistance be given for the realization of such, and favourable treatment be accorded to all Japanese enterprisers in connection with their making necessary arrangements such as employment of intellectual as well as manual labourers, equipments for transportation (railways, harbours, ships, etc.) and other needed establishments.

(5) All applications or requests from Japanese nationals be treated in friendly spirit.

II. VARIOUS ENTERPRISES

(1) Mining.

Permission for the exploration and/or exploitation of various minerals in the regions (including the areas reserved for the Government), which are desired by Japanese nationals for such purpose, be given as promptly and extensively as possible.

(2) Fishery.

It is requested that the fishing by Japanese nationals in the territorial waters be permitted, so far as it does not cause competition with the native fishery, and that an increase in number of fishing boats, fishermen and employees, necessary for the operation of the territorial-waters fishery mentioned above, as well as for that of deep-sea fishery by Japanese nationals, be allowed, and that various fisheries at or near the fishery bases and such establishments as necessary for the operation and the management of fisheries (fish-markets, ice-manufacturing factories, cold-storage houses, oil-tanks, factories for manufactured goods of fish, repair-shops for fishing boats, etc.) be permitted, and that the restriction on import-harbours for fish be abolished, and that the fish caught by the Japanese fishermen in the Netherlands-Indies be exempted from the import duties.

III. TRAFFIC AND COMMUNICATION.

(1) Opening of air-service between Japan and the Netherlands-Indies.

The establishment of a direct air-service between Japan and the Netherlands-Indies by Japanese planes be permitted and, in connection therewith, facilities necessary for wireless communication and meteorological information by wireless be rendered to Japanese aviators.

(2) Abolition of various restrictions on Japanese ships.

    (a) With regard to the coastal navigation already granted to the Japanese nationals by the Netherlands-Indies Government, an increase in number of Japanese ships be permitted, and the restrictions on the tonnage and navigable areas for the Japanese ships be abolished.

    (b) Permission for the coastal navigation be given to Japanese ships when necessary for the operation of Japanese enterprises.

    (c) Harbours, of which direct connection with Japan is desirable, for the promotion of the traffic and trade between Japan and the Netherlands-Indies, be designated as open-ports.

    (d) Formalities concerning the visit of Japanese ships to non-open-ports, which is necessary for the shipment of products destined for Japan, be simplified and dealt with as promptly as possible, and restrictions on the tonnage of the ships calling at non-open-ports be abolished.

(3) Improvement of the means of communication between Japan and the Netherlands-Indies.

    (a) In order to establish a stable and highly efficient means of communication between Japan and the Netherlands-Indies, consent be given to the laying of submarine cables between the two countries under the Japanese management, which are technically most up-to-date.

    (b) The prohibition of the use of Japanese language in the telegraphic communication between Japan and the Netherlands-Indies be removed.

IV. BUSINESS REGULATION.

    Applications by Japanese nationals regarding the business of warehousing, printing, weaving, ice manufacture, rubber smoking, etc., such as subjected to the Business Regulation Ordinance (Bedrijfs-reglementeerings-ordonnantie), be complied with as far as possible.

V. COMMERCE AND TRADE.

(1) Import-quotas for Japanese goods be arranged as mentioned in the list which will be annexed hereto.

(2) Japan is prepared to purchase the Netherlands-Indies products as mentioned in the list which will be annexed hereto.

(3) Increased percentage of import-quotas be allotted to the Japanese importers in the Netherlands-Indies.

(4) The Japanese importers in the Netherlands-Indies be exempted from the obligation to import the goods of third countries.

(5) With regard to the Japanese goods to be imported into the Netherlands-Indies, friendly measures be taken regarding the customs-tariff and customs formalities.

Although it was beyond any shadow of doubt that these contentions and demands would have to be denied almost *in toto*, it was decided not to bar the road to further negotiation outright. A memorandum, containing an outline of general policy as seen from the Netherland point of view and a few proposals for discussion, was composed by the Netherland delegation and would have been given to Mr. Yoshizawa in about a week's time, if Japanese politics had not interfered. In a speech made in the Diet on 21st January Mr. Matsuoka, the Japanese Minister of Foreign Affairs, asserted that for all practical purposes the Netherlands Indies were already included in the Greater East Asia Co-prosperity Sphere, under the leadership of Imperial Japan. The speech was widely advertised and could not be ignored without completely confusing public opinion in the Indies. To counteract its effect the Netherland Minister in Tokyo, on the 31st of January, delivered a statement at the Gaimusho in which the Netherland Government made it clear that they rejected any suggestion of having the Netherlands Indies incorporated in a new order in Asia under the leadership of any Power whatsoever, and that they could never be expected to let their actions be guided by the spirit of such a conception or to acquiesce in the consequences of its eventual application. After this had been done and published the memorandum was handed to the Japanese delegation on the 3rd of February. It revealed an attitude very much opposed to Japanese presumptions.

Memorandum presented by the Netherland delegation on 3rd February 1941.

In order to clarify the position of the Netherlands Indies with regard to the present economic negotiations and to avoid any possible misunderstandings, the Netherlands delegation would like to restate briefly the considerations determining the economic policy of the Netherlands Indies.

Whereas the improvement and adjustment of economic relations and the increase of mutual trade with neutral or non-belligerent countries is the object of a constant care, exercised in the spirit of goodwill, the measures taken in this respect must comply with the following principles.

In the first place it must be taken into consideration that the welfare, the progress and the emancipation of the population of the Netherlands Indies are the prime objects of the policy of the Netherlands Government. Measures, which would tend to run counter to the interests of the inhabitants, or which would unduly narrow the scope of their future development, should therefore be obviated.

In the second place the interests of the Netherlands Indies demand that the economic relations with foreign countries shall be maintained on a basis of strict non-discrimination; that the participation of such countries in the economic growth shall not disturb the gradual formation of the Netherlands Indies as a self-sustaining economic unit within the larger limits of the Kingdom; and that no preponderance shall be created of foreign interests in any field of economic activity.

In the third place it must be observed that, for the duration of the war in which the Kingdom of the Netherlands is involved, it is unavoidable that trade and other economic activities will be subject to restrictions preventing direct or indirect advantage to the enemy or safeguarding the defence of the Netherlands Indies.

Furthermore, in so far as the two opening paragraphs of the Japanese Delegation seem to imply, firstly, that the natural resources of the Netherlands Indies have been inadequately developed and, secondly, that the economic relations between Japan and the Netherlands Indies are of such an important and vital nature as to warrant the use of the term " interdependence," the Netherlands Delegation begs to point out that such contentions would not seem to be substantiated by the facts.

The fact that a considerable part of the so-called Buitengewesten is sparsely populated is primarily accountable, not to any lack of funds, labor or enterprising spirit, but to the relative scantiness and the scattered character of their natural resources. The poor results of several agricultural, forestry and mining enterprises, both domestic and foreign, in this part of the Netherlands Indies confirm this view, as is the case with the data, supplied by numerous scientific explorations.

As a whole, the Netherlands Indies not only provide practically all their own food, but in almost every field of agricultural activity, suited for the tropics, production has been developed to such an extent that restrictions had to be imposed to prevent a permanent glut in the markets of the world. Mineral production is relatively high, compared with mineral reserves, and in cases where the minerals found are of poor quality—as is the case with iron ore— exploitation was nevertheless undertaken as soon as a demand for these minerals could be expected to arise.

This does not mean that there is no room for further development. However, although the co-operation of *bona fide* private foreign capital and knowledge is welcomed within the limits delineated above, this development should proceed along lines of rational economy and should be realized mainly with the aid and to the benefit of the abundant population in other parts of the Netherlands Indies and of the fast increasing number of well-schooled and well-trained people among them. The fact that the number of government-organized agricultural emigrants from Java has reached the level of 50,000 persons a year and is rapidly increasing should by itself carry the conviction that the Netherlands Indies do not stand in need of immigration from foreign countries and that all parts of the Buitengewesten, where cultivation of the soil offers some economic prospect, are necessary for the alleviation of the pressure of the population in Java and elsewhere.

As regards the importance of trade relations between the Netherlands Indies and the Japanese Empire, it should be borne in mind that the share of the Japanese Empire in the total export-value of the Netherlands Indies decreased from an average of 4.21 % in 1930-1932 to an average of 3.74 % in 1937-1939. It is true that the share of Japan in the imports of the Netherlands Indies was larger, but it should not be overlooked that these imports were to a great extent made possible through the creation of buying power by exports from the Netherlands Indies to third countries.

It is a memorable fact that the share of China (including Hongkong) and Manchukuo in the export-value of the Netherlands Indies shows an even more adverse development, falling from 8.15 % in 1930-1932 to 3.55 % in 1937-1939. Even the present war, though it gradually cut off most of the European markets, did but slightly alter the situation, the above percentages for January-November 1940 being for the Japanese Empire 5·18 % and for China and Manchukuo 3·94%.

The export situation proves that the welfare of the Netherlands Indies depends on its trade with the world as a whole and that mere geographical propinquity is not the governing element in the creation or the maintenance of a voluminous trade. In fact prosperity in and consequent demand from the importing countries are much more important elements than distance.

The figures undoubtedly show that there is room for improvement and there is every reason to further the normal development of economic relations as much as possible. With regard to this the Netherlands Delegation avail themselves of the opportunity that economic negotiations have been initiated by the Japanese Government to offer the following proposals :

1. Imports in Japan of products from the Netherlands Indies.
    Netherlands Indian products, economically important to the Netherlands Indies, the entrance of which in Japan is now barred by monetary and other measures, be purchased for home consumption in Japan. Among others this regards specially :
    (a) Sugar, a considerable shortage of which exists in Japan and those regions of China and Manchukuo, which used to be provided with sugar by Japanese refineries.[1]
    (b) Coffee, a reasonable share in the imports of which be granted to the Netherlands Indies.
2. Free use of yen balances.
    Yen balances accruing to Netherlands nationals or companies in Japan be made available for any lawful transaction appertaining to the economic intercourse between Japan and the Netherlands Indies.
3. Freedom of business.
    Netherlands nationals and companies in Japan be granted the necessary liberty for the undisturbed exercise of their trade.

With the lists cleared in this manner the prospects of a continued tug-of-war could be better reviewed. Again, Japanese politics provided time for a thorough examination.

[1] These refineries used to obtain a substantial part of their raw sugar from Java.

A Japanese Government spokesman explained to the foreign Press that the Netherland declaration of disinterestedness *vis-à-vis* the new order would not affect in the least Japan's fixed resolve to carry on the negotiations with the Netherlands Indies, intimating serious doubt concerning the legal status of the Netherland Government in London, which was but a tool in British hands. The manipulators of the puppet regime apparently saw puppet regimes all over the world. This totally false impression, however, had to be set right before things could go on ; it was unacceptable for a Netherland delegation to treat with people who did not acknowledge and respect their principals. The deadlock lasted until the end of February, when satisfactory explanations from the Japanese side, throwing the blame—as usual—on incorrect Press reports, at last enabled the delegation to proceed.

Under ordinary circumstances the Japanese memorandum would almost certainly have led directly to a final disagreement, but the circumstances were not normal and it might be important to avoid an open rupture. The war situation was not encouraging. Victory seemed a long way off ; Russia remained a problem picture ; active participation by the United States could hardly be expected for quite a time to come. War with Japan might invite such participation, but even then there was a great difference in preparedness on both sides and the loss, even the temporary loss, of the Indies would gravely damage the strategic and the supply position of the Allies. From this point of view everything pleaded for a policy of gaining time.

The crucial question remained, whether Japan intended aggressive action in the near future. The prevailing uncertainty in this respect probably extended to the council chamber of the Japanese Government of the period. There can be no doubt that the military and naval staffs were continuously planning, training, and equipping ; there were signs of an infiltration into Southern Indo-China, and at about this time the Japanese merchant navy began its slow retirement from the high seas. But there must have been many problems : the attitude and the needs of the Axis partners, the neutrality of Russia, the rapidity of reaction in the United States. Then the question would arise how much could be gained by bluster and blackmail, without the actual use of force. The Government in power was still of the intermediate type, aggressive in its aims, but hesitant about ways and means. These considerations pointed in the same direction : to gain time might be essential.

And, lastly, nobody could quite foretell the changes of alignment the war might still provoke. Under these conditions it seemed advisable to keep open the way to some sort of agreement. With the interminable fighting in China on her hands, Japan might find herself faced one day by so many adversaries that war would appear precarious even to the most arrogant of her war lords. The chances were decidedly thin, but if such a situation came to pass a justified fear of strangulation might impede an otherwise possible peaceful settlement. And if she did not want war, history has taught us that Japan can retreat from almost any position provided the secret is guarded and she does not too openly lose face.

But if there were cogent reasons for continuing the negotiations, it was fully appreciated that the road was sown with mines and traps. Public opinion in the Indies and elsewhere was excited and full of suspicion. Many could not understand how negotiations were possible with a country that had openly allied itself to the cause of the enemy. Facts that leaked out concerning the Japanese demands, and fancies spun by the inevitable " well-informed persons," increased the misgivings and the general scepticism. The delicate situation imposed a reserve that hampered public justification. The examples of Indo-China and Thailand distorted the view and the judgment of many. Minor incidents acquired an ominous meaning. And the growing hysteria of the Japanese Press, under Government inspiration, broadcasting alternate boasts, threats, and incriminations, necessitated almost con-

tinuous vigilance and counteraction. Only the public confidence in the Government, the steadfast support and trust
of the Volksraad—the Netherlands Indies' chamber of
representatives—which was kept confidentially informed, and
the invaluable work of half a dozen able foreign newspaper
correspondents helped to prevent a premature breakdown
from these causes.

Furthermore, as the months went by the hope of maintaining the peace evaporated. Japan was slowly but per-
sistently strengthening and securing her base for attack.
Already in the first stage of the conversations ensuing from
the related exchange of memoranda, the Netherland delegation
had to caution their Japanese opponents that a Japanese
occupation of Southern Indo-China would constitute a
military menace towards the Netherlands Indies of such a
seriousness that it would cancel any agreement reached in
the economic sphere. Between March and May 1941 Mr.
Matsuoka made his European tour and returned full of admiration for the Axis and with a Russo-Japanese Neutrality
Pact in his pocket. As Japan installed herself ever more
firmly in Indo-China and Thailand the potential leak in the
blockade of Germany widened. The two countries together
produced 130,000 tons of rubber annually as against a Japanese
consumption in past years of 50,000 tons ; her need for
10,000 tons of tin per annum was exceeded by at least 50 per
cent. in the production of her new sphere of influence. Here
were possible surpluses that might easily find their way to
Germany along the Siberian route ; it began to seem sheer
suicide to add to these quantities from Malaya and the Netherlands Indies, where Japan had bought her supplies in more
normal times. And the growing conviction that Japan was
planning an early attack, and that every ton of material
shipped to her would be used to push forward that attack,
went a long way to vindicate that " stiffening attitude " of
the Netherland delegation which was so loudly decried by
the Japanese Press. What had seemed reasonable in June

1940 began to look extremely dangerous in 1941, and although the proviso about the exigencies of war had been consistently made from the beginning, it was difficult to make the Japanese accept its consequences to their own disadvantage.

The third drawback of continuing the negotiations was the continued presence of the Japanese delegation and their numerous staff. It began to look like a permanent mission, and the Japanese certainly toyed with the idea. It very obviously was a permanent source of information for their plotting Army and Navy headquarters, and the constant changes of personnel provided them regularly with messengers travelling under diplomatic immunities. The moment would come when the benefits of gaining time would be outweighed by the capacity for mischief and nuisance of this inquisitive company.

The picture would not be complete without some further remarks on the personalities of Mr. Yoshizawa and Mr. Ishizawa. Mr. Yoshizawa, careful and slow of speech, showed a well-balanced and strong, if somewhat formalistic character throughout. So far as could be ascertained he reported quite clearly and fairly on the situation and the Netherland attitude, and he was greatly vexed by the explosive tactics of his chief, Mr. Matsuoka. He became convinced that Japan should either accept the Netherland proposals or make war, and that all those threats and rantings about co-prosperity served no useful purpose. His leanings may have been towards peace ; although he was painfully conscious of the inevitable failure of his mission, his equanimity remained undisturbed to the end.

Mr. Ishizawa was more of a prima donna : exultant one day and despondent the next. However, he liked the Indies and was not aggressively minded, and he, too, strove to understand why the Netherland delegation acted as they did. If the negotiations lasted longer than seemed possible under impossible conditions and were broken off in an almost amiable manner, the two Japanese protagonists had their share in the achievement.

The conversations started on the last days of February and were conducted from the Netherland side with infinite patience and great ability by Mr. Van Hoogstraten; his Japanese opposite was Mr. Ishizawa. They covered the whole field, including the requests for oil concessions, which had been entered by Mr. Mukai. There were the endless explanations and reiterations that seem unavoidable in cases of difference of opinion with the Japanese. But although on almost every point there had to be refusals and drastic retrenchments of the Japanese requests, they showed peculiarly little fight or even resistance and mitigated their demands almost at the first frown. The area of the coveted oil concessions was reduced from 17·5 million hectares to 1·7 million hectares without so much as the batting of an eyelid, and even when it was made clear that only a concession of 0·3 million hectares could be taken into consideration as a first instalment, they hardly offered a protest. It was difficult to account for this change of attitude.

The explanation probably is to be found in a complexity of circumstances. Mr. Ishizawa must have realized from the outset how impossible the demands were for a self-respecting country. They had in all likelihood been designed by the first delegation on instructions from Tokyo; to alter them did not hurt his author's pride. The Japanese military were kept very busy in Indo-China; they would not object to some soft-pedalling in the intractable Indies. The exploratory conversations between Mr. Cordell Hull and Admiral Nomura had only just begun in Washington; the spotlight on this main stage put the wings in the shadow. And, maybe, Mr. Ishizawa saw a chance, so indispensable to the feelings of every Japanese negotiator, of accomplishing at least a modicum of success. It would always mean introducing the thin edge of the wedge.

For a time the prospects were more promising than they had been yet. But then the necessities of economic warfare clouded the horizon. It became more and more certain that essential war materials were reaching Germany from the Far East. The licensing system for exports, introduced long ago to safeguard the home market of the Netherlands Indies under war conditions, was rapidly extended to cover all the important supplies; quota to non-allied countries were increasingly cut. Consequently during the last weeks of these conversations the whole dispute seemed to centre around the exports of rubber and tin.

In the course of the negotiations the Japanese had raised their figures for those commodities to 30,000 and 12,500 tons to be purchased in the Netherlands Indies annually. Licenses for the exportation of 10,000 and 2,300 tons respectively had already been granted for the first six months of 1941. The general situation warranted, in the judgment of the Netherland Government, a complete discontinuation of these exports, but policy seemed to recommend a slightly more gradual stoppage. Malaya had already drastically cut her deliveries to Japan. Although the Japanese were willing to reduce the figures of their requirements to the original 20,000 tons for rubber and 3,000 tons for tin, they could not agree to any further reduction. They denied that they were providing the Germans with these materials and offered a guarantee that the rubber and tin from the Netherlands Indies would be used only in Japan itself. Of course this guarantee was valueless, but it took some diplomacy to say so without offence. An assurance that the quota eventually allowed for 1941 would be continued in following years had to be denied, as the Netherland Government needed a free hand in conducting the blockade.

The exact determination of the Netherland attitude was greatly facilitated at this juncture by a short visit to the Netherlands Indies of two members of the Cabinet in London : Dr. E. N. van Kleffens, Minister of Foreign Affairs, and Mr. Ch. J. I. M. Welter, at that time Minister of the Colonies. Their temporary presence in Batavia served to confirm the unity of purpose and policy that existed between the Netherland Government and public opinion in the Netherlands Indies. It also increased public confidence, but those who could look behind the scenes could not but realize both the strength and the weakness of what was then beginning to be known as the A—B—C—D front. Its strength was in the general resolve to withstand further Japanese aggression; its weakness appeared in the lack of definite mutual commitments and the deplorable inadequacy of co-ordination in the military preparations for the defence. Once again the machinery of democracy failed to gear its speed of action to the rapidly developing operations of a totalitarian aggressor. Delaying tactics and individual tenacity of resistance in peace and war seemed the only possibility in the first stages of the conflict.

At last, however, there was nothing more to be said. Mr. Matsuoka was back in Japan, bringing the Russo-Japanese Neutrality Pact, and had given his final instructions. On 14th May the Japanese delegation presented their revised proposals, but the tables annexed to them were not forthcoming until 22nd May. The text follows below with the exception of tables I and II, which contained nothing but a fantastic and elaborate last minute claim for a share of somewhere between 75 and 100 per cent. for Japan in the main imports of the Netherlands Indies. This preposterous request, however, carried no weight in the ultimate disagreement.

Memorandum presented by the Japanese delegation
on 14th/22nd May 1941.

In reconsideration of the memorandum, which the Japanese Delegation presented to the Netherlands Delegation on the 16th Jan. 1941, they herein present to the Netherlands Delegation the following new proposal. They wish to make it clear, however, that the Japanese viewpoint expressed in the preamble of the above-mentioned memorandum is firmly held by the Japanese Government.

I. THE ENTRY OF JAPANESE NATIONALS.

(a) With regard to the entry of Japanese employees, when employers concerned apply for labour permits for their employees, the Government of the Netherlands Indies will give favourable consideration for speedy granting of as many permits as possible, as far as circumstances allow, within the limits of existing regulations, and the permits to be granted will be at least 1,600 per annum.

(b) Employees, for whom their employees apply for labour permits in order to replace existing employees, and employees for whom their employees apply for the extention of labour permits, and those whose purpose of entry is of temporary nature, are not included in the number cited above in the paragraph (a).

(c) In consideration of the necessity in various districts, the Government of the Netherlands Indies will permit, as a whole, a certain number of Japanese doctors (including dentists) to enter the Netherlands Indies, if their object is to practise medical treatment solely to Japanese residents.

It is also understood that Japanese doctors (including dentists) who are permitted to practise medical treatment to Japanese employees working for Japanese enterprises in outer regions, can extend their medical treatment, when necessary, to employees or servants of other nationalities working in the same enterprises.

II. ENTERPRISE AND BUSINESS.

Whenever Japanese nationals concerned submit concrete applications for consent or permission for establishment or extention, etc., of various enterprises and businesses, either in own account or in joint account with Netherlands enterprisers, the Government of the Netherlands Indies will give favourable consideration to the said applications and, as far as there are no special obstacles owing to the reasons of national defence or to the necessity of reservation for the subjects of the Netherlands Indies, they will allow previous investigations, which are deemed necessary for the execution of their plans, and will give consent or permission for the said establishment or extention, etc.

When the said consent or permission has once been given, the Government of the Netherlands Indies will give favourable treatment and necessary facilities as much as possible for the engagement of employees, the building up of transportation equipments and other needed establishments, etc.

(a) With regard to the mining, when Japanese enterprisers apply for the permission for exploration and exploitation of mineral resources, the Government of the Netherlands Indies will give favourable consideration thereto and will grant required permission, as far as there are no special obstacles.

The same will be the case when Japanese enterprisers apply for the permission for exploration or exploitation according to article 5A of the Mining Law in order to participate in the mining within the area reserved for the Government.

(b) With regard to the fishery, when concrete applications for permission are submitted by Japanese nationals concerned, the Government of the Netherlands Indies will grant permission, provided that there are no special obstacles owing to the reasons of national defence or to the necessity of reservation for the subjects of the Netherlands Indies, especially for the natives, and they will give favourable treatment and necessary facilities for the engagement of employees working for Japanese fisheries as well as for the establishment of accessory installations necessary for the operation of the said fisheries, etc.

(c) With regard to commercial and other businesses, when applications are submitted by Japanese nationals, the Government of the Netherlands Indies will grant permission, provided that there are no special obstacles, and also concerning warehouse-business and others, which are already subjected to the Business Regulation Ordinance, they will give favourable consideration to each case, when concrete applications are submitted and they will grant permission, provided that there are no special obstacles.

III. TRAFFIC AND COMMUNICATION.

(a) From the viewpoint that the development of air services between Japan and the Netherlands Indies will greatly contribute to the strengthening of economic relations between both countries, the Government of the Netherlands Indies will, at a suitable opportunity in the future, co-operate with the Japanese Government for the opening of direct air service between Japan and the Netherlands Indies, but, for the time being, will co-operate with the Japanese Government for the improvement of connection between Japanese and Netherlands aeroplanes at Bangkok, Saigon and other places.

(b) With regard to the telegraphic communication between Japan and the Netherlands Indies, the Government of the Netherlands Indies will cooperate with the Japanese Government for laying of technically most up-to-date submarine cables under Japanese management, in order to establish a safe and efficient means of communication, at a suitable opportunity in the future, but, for the time being, they will cooperate with the Japanese

Government for the improvement of the radiotelegraphic connection between Malabar and Japan as well as for the utilization of the submarine cable between Yap and Menado.

(c) With regard to the coastal navigation, when applications are submitted timely by existing Japanese enterprisers, who feel the necessity of their own coastal navigation owing to the growth of their enterprises, and also when applications are submitted at the beginning as a part of their whole plans by new Japanese enterprisers, who foresee the necessity of their own coastal navigation, the Government of the Netherlands Indies will grant permission, provided that there are no special obstacles owing to the reasons of national defence.

The Government of the Netherlands Indies state that, with regard to the coastal navigation already permitted to Japanese nationals, when Japanese nationals concerned, feeling the necessity of the increase in number of or in tonnage of ships, apply for the permission for the said increase, they will grant permission, provided that there are no special obstacles, and they further state that they have no intention to make difficult the navigation and the coastal trade of the ship, which is already permitted to engage herself in the said businesses.

(d) When Japanese nationals concerned, feeling the necessity to have certain closed ports opened for special products or for general trade, in accordance with the development of Japanese enterprises or the increase of products or the furtherance of trade between Japan and the Netherlands Indies, apply for the permission for opening of those closed ports, the Government of the Netherlands Indies will grant permission, provided that there are no special obstacles.

(e) When Japanese nationals concerned, feeling the necessity of Japanese ships to call at closed ports for the shipment of products destined for Japan, apply for permission to that end, the Government of the Netherlands Indies will grant permission provided that there are no special obstacles, and they will treat the matter as promptly as possible.

IV.   Trade and Commerce.

The Government of the Netherlands Indies state that, in view of the circumstances that the demand of Japanese industries on the products of the Netherlands Indies is rapidly increasing and the increasing import of Japanese articles will contribute towards the promotion of the welfare of the people of the Netherlands Indies, they recognize the importance of the position Japan is now occupying and will occupy in the future in the foreign trade of the Netherlands Indies, and will take the following measures to be effected for one year ending . . ., 1942.

1. (*a*) The quotas and or the percentages as shown in the attached tables I and II shall be allotted to articles to be imported from Japan into the Netherlands Indies,

(*b*) Japanese importers in the Netherlands Indies shall be given import percentages ranging from ten to thirty percents according to the kinds of articles.

2. Unconditional and prompt permission shall be given for the exportation to Japan of the products of the Netherlands Indies mentioned in the attached list.

3. With regard to the import duties, export taxes, surtaxes and official prices (including the prices in the Price List), not only no discriminatory treatment shall be given to the articles imported from and or exported to Japan, but also favourable treatment shall be accorded to them.

V. In case neither the Government of Japan nor the Government of the Netherlands Indies will give notice to terminate the above-cited measures three months before the expiration of the period of one year as mentioned above, the said measures will continue to be operative for successive years, unless notice will be given three months before the expiration of each year.

TABLE III

Description of articles.	*Quantity in* 1,000 *kg.*
1. Coffee	480
2. Wood	65,000
3. Ebony with white streaks	340
4. Dammar and Copal	1,450
5. Kapok fibre (including kapok fibre in the seed) .	1,000
6. Kapok seed and Cotton seed .	5,500
7. Indian corn	80,000
8. Copra	25,000
9. Cassava-root	8,000
10. Rattan	1,000
11. Palm oil	12,000

TABLE III.—*Continued*

Description of articles.	Quantity in 1,000 kg.
12. Scrap iron (including scrap of tinned steel sheets)	60,000
13. Cotton	1,600
14. Tanning materials	4,000
15. Sugar	100,000
16. Rubber	20,000
17. Tin	
18. Tin ore (containing 73 % or more tin by weight)	3,000
19. Bauxite	400,000
20. Nickel ore	180,000
21. Manganese ore	20,000
22. Salt	100,000
23. Castor seed	6,000
24. Cinchona bark	600
25. Quinine	80
26. Mineral Oil	1,800,000

The Government of the Netherlands Indies are requested to make, through their influence, the oil companies concerned to increase the quantity of export of mineral oil to Japan up to 3,800,000 tons per annum by providing means of increasing production, by appropriating quantities, if any, which are allocated to countries other than Japan but are rendered undeliverable, or by any other means.

The Government of Japan are prepared to purchase mineral oil from the Netherlands Indies up to 3,800,000 tons per year for the duration of at least five years and request that the Government of the Netherlands Indies will prevail upon the oil companies to enable them to make new contracts with Japan for quantities considerable larger than those in the present contracts.

27. Pitch cokes	25,000
28. Jute (refined)	1,300
29. Molasses	60,000

30. Beeswax . . . . . ⎫
31. Beans and pease . . . . ⎬ Value in 1000 yen
32. Cocoa . . . . . ⎪   800
33. Shells of mollusca . . ⎭
34. Amorphophallus tubers . .

35. The Government of the Netherlands Indies are requested to take positive measures for promoting the export of scrap iron, molybdenum ore, chrome iron ore, wolfram ore and mica (high quality) to Japan.

                                                    In 1,000 kg.
36. Sisal fibre   40,000

N.B.—In view of the wishes of the Netherlands Delegation expressed in the memorandum of the 3rd February 1941, about the imports to Japan of the products from the Netherlands Indies, especially sugar and coffee, the Japanese Delegation will advise the Japanese Government to increase the imports of the said products as more as possible than the quantities mentioned above, if the reply from the Netherlands Delegation to the Japanese memorandum of the 14th May 1941, will be favourable.

Again the Japanese Government managed to render a prompt answer by the Netherland delegation impossible. Even before the annexes of the Japanese memorandum had been completed, Mr. Matsuoka applied, through the British Ambassador in Tokyo, for the good offices of the British Government in order to induce the Netherland Government to raise the rubber quota. As the interests of both Governments ran entirely parallel, his chances of success were negligible, but the request necessitated a consultation on the question, whether a three-cornered discussion on this aspect of the joint blockade might ease the strain. It was decided otherwise, but before the decision was reached several days had gone by. And in the meantime Mr. Matsuoka had turned on the heat in the Japanese Press and in the comments of his spokesman. There were dire threats, accusations of insincerity and malingering, doubts expressed about the integrity of intentions. Again the long-suffering Netherland Minister had to lodge a protest; and not until 6th June could the answering memorandum be handed to Mr. Yoshizawa in an atmosphere of great public excitement. It was orally explained to him that the answer was to be considered as final. He read it straight away and could not refrain from showing some disappointment; the reasons will be found in the following text.

Memorandum presented by the Netherland delegation on 6th June 1941.

Preamble

From the memoranda, presented by the Japanese economic delegation on May 14th and 22nd 1941, the Netherland delegation have noticed with satisfaction that the Japanese proposals have been modified in several instances after the thorough discussion of the various points at issue in the course of the negotiations. They value these modifications as a result of the endeavours of the Japanese delegation to adapt the Japanese proposals, as originally formulated, to the exigencies of the present abnormal circumstances, and to meet to a certain extent the objections raised by the Netherland delegation on account of the incompatibility of a number of those proposals with the principles of economic policy in the Netherlands Indies.

Nevertheless the Netherland delegation cannot but express their regret that the views of the Japanese Government are still materially at variance with these principles.

In fact the Japanese memorandum of the 14th of May 1941 states that the Japanese Government still firmly hold the views expressed in the preamble of the memorandum of the 16th of January 1941. As these views were based on a supposed inadequacy in the development of the natural resources of the Netherlands Indies and an assumed interdependence between this country and the Japanese Empire, it is clear that their practical application would tend to create a special position for the Japanese interests in the Netherlands Indies.

It seems therefore appropriate to point once more to the fundamental economic policy of the Netherland Government in regard to this archipelago, as set forth in the Netherland memorandum of February 3rd 1941; a policy, which involves the furtherance of welfare, progress and emancipation of its population, non-discrimination towards friendly foreign powers and the avoidance of the creation of preponderance of foreign interests in any particular field of activity.

This country has reached a stage of economic growth in which, with the assistance of the mother country, it may be deemed capable in the main of adequately developing its own economic life and resources. This process is in harmony with the aspirations of the population and care should be taken not to hamper its course by too liberal an admittance of foreign interests.

The density of the population in Java and other parts of the archipelago, as well as the density of the population in the mother country, emphasize still more the need to open up the economic resources and to reserve the labour market of this country as much as possible for the benefit of the subjects of the Kingdom.

On the other hand this policy implies that foreign enterprises, once established in the Netherlands Indies, are subject to the same rules and entitled to the same facilities as national enterprises of a similar nature, provided that the interests of Netherland subjects in the country of origin of those enterprises are treated in the same spirit.

Apart from these considerations of general economic policy, the relations between the Netherlands Indies and other countries must, for the duration of the war, be affected by the subjection of trade and other economic activities to certain unavoidable restrictions, in order to prevent direct or indirect advantage to the enemy, to safeguard the defence of the Netherlands Indies, and to promote the war effort of the Kingdom and its allies. These restrictions are, by their nature, of a temporary character.

Notwithstanding the difference in general conception, which appears to separate the two governments, the Netherland delegation remain desirous to make another effort to convince the Japanese delegation not only of the reasonableness of the position taken by the Netherland Government in regard to the specific questions raised in the recent Japanese memoranda, but also of the practical possibilities open to the Japanese interests on various points.

To this end the views of the Netherland Government in respect to each of these questions are set forth here below.

I. THE ENTRY OF JAPANESE NATIONALS.

a. The purpose of the Foreign Labour Ordinance is to reserve employment in the Netherlands Indies as far as possible for the inhabitants of the country. Consequently labour permits can only be granted to foreigners if their labour is deemed necessary and no Netherland subjects are available for the specific position. Furthermore, it is understood that the employer concerned shall, as far as possible, provide adequate practical training for Netherland subjects to fill future vacancies. The need of foreign employment is always estimated in a liberal way, a policy, which will be continued. The Netherland Government aim at an expeditious handling of applications for labour permits as far as is feasible in connection with the necessity to obtain advice from the different authorities concerned and, in some cases, of local investigation.

Because of the vital interests involved the Netherland Government do not see their way to give an assurance that in a number of cases labour permits would be granted to foreigners without taking into account the basic principles of the ordinance. Therefore the unconditional guarantee of admission of Japanese nationals up to the full quota, as asked for in the Japanese memorandum, which moreover would constitute an inadmissible discrimination against other foreign countries, can not be given.

b. In this connection the question, as to whether the granting of certain labour permits should or should not be included in the aforementioned quota, does not seem to need further discussion.

c. The Netherland Government are willing to give favourable consideration to a change in the existing regulations in order to permit a strictly limited number of Japanese doctors to enter the Netherlands Indies for medical practice, solely amongst Japanese residents, in those places where the number of Japanese residents would justify such a course. An extension of their medical practice to all employees or servants working for Japanese enterprises is not appropriate, as the majority of those employees and servants consists of people of non-Japanese origin.

II.   ENTERPRISE AND BUSINESS.

The establishment of enterprises of foreigners in their own account or in joint account with Netherland nationals is permitted, provided such enterprise, in the opinion of the authorities concerned, will constitute a fitting contribution to the economic development of the country within the scope of the general economic policy referred to in the preamble.

a. The foregoing also prevails for the participation by foreigners in mining enterprises in the Netherlands Indies.

The answer to the requests, made by the Japanese economic delegation with reference to participation by Japanese interests in the exploration and exploitation of mineral oil products in the Netherlands Indies, will be found in the first annex of this memorandum.

b. As the extension of fisheries and fishing industries should be reserved mainly for the native population, the Netherland Government do not find themselves in a position to grant permits or facilities for fishing to foreigners. Whether under special circumstances there might be a possibility of granting such facilities to certain foreign applicants will have to be considered separately in each case, judging every request on its own merits. For obvious reasons of national defence the Netherland Government will, for the time being, not be able to grant such facilities.

c. What has been said heretofore about the participation of foreigners in enterprises in the Netherlands Indies also stands for the " commercial and other business," as well as for the " warehouse business and others " meant in Paragraph II sub *c* of the Japanese memorandum. It is necessary to reserve these branches of activity to a large extent for Netherland subjects on account of the fact that especially in smaller commercial and other enterprises, like shops, small warehouses and small factories, opportunities can be found for the commercial and industrial education of the rural masses, which is one of the main problems of economic policy for the Netherland Government.

III. TRAFFIC AND COMMUNICATION.

a. The Netherland Government will be pleased to co-operate with the Japanese Government for the improvement of the connection between Japanese and Netherland airlines at Bangkok, Saigon and possibly other places. They are, however, of opinion that the future development of air transport within the archipelago and with foreign countries depends on so many uncertain factors that under the present circumstances they could not commit themselves on this subject.

b. Taking into account the present development of wireless connections there is, as far as the Netherland Government can see, no motive for the duplication of telegraphic communication between Japan and the Netherlands Indies by expensive submarine cables. In case an improvement of the radio communication between Malabar and Japan might prove necessary, the Netherland Government will be pleased to give the co-operation required. There is no indication that, in addition to this radio communication, provisions need be made for the utilization of the submarine cable between Yap and Menado, which, moreover, is in such a bad state of repair that for its use extensive and costly renovations and improvements would be required.

c. Coastal navigation in the Netherlands Indies has in principle been prohibited for ships under foreign flag in order to promote and protect national shipping. The exceptions to this rule, which have been made in certain cases—including certain ships under the Japanese flag—should be regarded as a maximum concession granted to shipping interests, which already existed when the present shipping laws came into force. The Netherland Government are ready, however, to continue granting such facilities to the concessionaires in coastal shipping under a foreign flag as are needed for the maintenance of their enterprises within the present limits of type, number and tonnage of ships.

d. The opening of closed ports for the export of special products or for general trade purposes depends on the proven needs of the regions concerned in connection with the available shipping. Each case will have to be decided on its own merits, and on a basis of strict nondiscrimination with regard to foreign flags.

e. The foregoing also applies to permissions for ships under a foreign flag to call at closed ports.

IV. TRADE AND COMMERCE.

As the prosperity of the Netherlands Indies depends, to a large extent, on trade with many countries, it is of vital importance that the Netherland Government retain, as far as possible, their freedom of action with regard to the adjustment of imports to the exigencies of the export situation.

Besides it is necessary, for the duration of the war, to exercise a strict control on imports in order to avoid waste of foreign currency, and on exports in order to prevent that exports from the Netherlands Indies should contribute in any way to provide the enemy with materials of strategic value. The Japanese Government will undoubtedly understand that the present struggle for national existence admits of no other course.

Apart from these considerations the quickly changing international situation renders it inadvisable to enter into formal and binding agreements concerning the importation or the exportation of definite quantities of commodities for any extended period of time. On the other hand, it is in accordance with the trade policy of the Netherland Government to refrain from abrupt changes, as long as the circumstances and the vital interests of the country permit. The Japanese Government may rest assured that this policy will be adhered to in respect of the mutually important trade between the Netherlands Indies and Japan.

1. (a) With regard to the Japanese interests in the Netherlands Indian import trade an agreement was reached after the fullest consideration and embodied in the so-called Hart-Ishizawa and Van Mook–Kotani agreements. The Netherland Government see no necessity to modify these agreements, which are still in force.

Under the present unsettled circumstances it seems impossible to enter into any commitment concerning the quantities of certain commodities, which will be imported from any particular country, even during the next twelve months. The Netherland Government are, however, prepared—if such is wished for by the Japanese Government in the interest of the regulation of production in Japan—to state the quantities of goods for which during the next six months permits will be issued for importation from countries at choice, on which permits importation from Japan will be possible as long as prices and terms of delivery can meet competition from other countries. These quantities will have to be determined according to the actual needs of the Netherlands Indies.

(b) The Netherland Government remain of the opinion that the position of Japanese importers in the Netherlands Indies has been satisfactorily settled on the basis of the abovementioned agreements, and that they could not, without causing undue harm to other interests concerned, enlarge this share.

2. The necessities of war render it impossible for the Netherland Government to enter into any obligation to grant permits unconditionally for the exportation of various commodities for as long a period as the next twelve months. Any statement of policy in this respect, even for a much shorter space of time, must be subject to the proviso that it cannot be binding whenever, in the judgment of the Netherland Government, the full execution would be of direct or indirect advantage to the enemy or harmful to the interests of the Kingdom and its allies.

As, however, the Netherland Government appreciate the difficulty for the Japanese Government to adjust their internal economic policy on a basis of complete uncertainty with regard to imports from the Netherlands Indies, the Netherland Government have no objection to state—under the express proviso mentioned heretofore—their intentions with regard to restrictions of exports for the year 1941 as determined by their view on the present situation. Such a statement is drafted in the second annex of this memorandum. It needs not be expressly mentioned in this connection that, although the Netherland Government must vindicate their right to be the sole judges of the exigencies of war with regard to exports, the ordinary channels of international intercourse remain open for the consideration of facts and complaints.

3. With regard to the import duties, export taxes, surtaxes and official prices the same treatment will be given to commodities imported from and exported to Japan, as to commodities imported from and exported to all other countries, in accordance with the principle of nondiscrimination.

V. Termination of Agreement.

If the present exchange of views would lead to the drawing up of an agreement the terminating clause could then be considered simultaneously with the wording of the document.

VI. Netherland Proposals.

The Netherland delegation propose that the following be adopted by the Japanese Government as their contribution to the furthering of the economic relations.

1. As a shortage of sugar is known to exist in the Japanese Empire and adjacent regions, the Japanese Government undertake to provide for the importation, during the remaining months of 1941, of Java sugar at a rate of 150,000 tons a year.

2. The amount of ebony to be imported into Japan from the Netherland Indies shall, for the same period, be brought to a level of 2,000 tons a year, which quantity yet only represents about 50 % of the normal imports.

3. The Japanese Government will provide for the importations, during the remaining months of 1941, of coffee from the Netherlands Indies at a rate of 1,000 tons a year.

4. The Japanese Government will take measures to make available all yen balances accruing to Netherland nationals or companies in Japan, for any lawful transaction appertaining to the economic intercourse between Japan and the Netherlands Indies.

5. The Japanese Government will grant to Netherland nationals and companies in Japan the necessary liberty for the undisturbed exercise of their trade, in a similar way as such liberty is granted to Japanese nationals and companies in the Netherlands Indies.

Annex I

The Netherland Government, considering the Mangkalihat peninsula as a sphere of interest of the B.O.M. for future extension, have no objection to grant the B.O.M. concessions for the exploration of 278,000 ha in the Sangkoelirang region, which form the subject of the application of that company of February 17th 1941.

The applications of the same date for exploration in the Banggai block and North-East-New-Guinea will be held over for consideration at such time when the activities of the B.O.M. shall be sufficiently developed to justify a further extension of its concessions. Before granting concessions in these areas to possible later applicants the Netherland Government will carefully examine the applications filed by the B.O.M.

Annex II

Concerning the exportation to Japan from the Netherlands Indies of the various commodities and quantities, specified in table III, annexed to the memorandum of the Japanese delegation of May 14th, the following can be stated.[1]

Under the present circumstances and unless the full execution of the measures to be mentioned below would, in their judgment, be of direct or indirect advantage to the enemy or harmful to the interests of the Kingdom and its allies, it is the intention of the Netherland Government for the year 1941:

a. To maintain or institute quota for the exportation of the following commodities mentioned in table III, to the Japanese Empire during the year 1941 in such a way that the total quantities in metric tons to be exported during that year can reach the figure opposed to each article:

16. Rubber	. . . . .	15,000
17/18. Tin and tin ore (in tin content)	.	3,000
20. Nickel ore	. . . . .	150,000
22. Castor seed	. . . . .	6,000
24. Cinchona bark	. . . .	600

b. To institute monthly quota for the exportation of the following commodities, mentioned in table III, to the Japanese Empire for the remaining months of 1941 to the amounts, specified in metric tons opposite each article:

[1] To avoid possible misunderstanding it is expressly observed that the following statement in no wise excludes the application of export regulations and quota to commodities *not* mentioned in table III.

4.	Damar and copal	.	.	.	125
5.	Kapok fibre (including kapok fibre in the seed)	.	.	.	100
6.	Kapok seed and cotton seed	.	.	500
8.	Copra (including the equivalent in cocoanut oil)	.	.	.	1,650
10.	Rattan	.	.	.	100
11.	Palm oil	.	.	.	1,000
14.	Tanning materials	.	.	.	125
19.	Bauxite	.	.	.	20,000
21.	Manganese ore	.	.	.	500
25.	Quinine (net weight)	.	.	.	5
28.	Jute (refined)	.	.	.	125

c. To refrain from instituting quota for the exportation to the Japanese Empire of the commodities, mentioned in table III but not included in the lists sub *a* and *b*, with the following reservations.

The export quotum fixed at present for scrap iron is to be regarded as a measure to prevent wholesale thefts of iron as a consequence of the high price obtained in case of unlimited export. Otherwise there is no objection to export to Japan the available scrap-iron, as far as it is not needed for home consumption or for the allies of the Netherlands.

Under the last-mentioned proviso there is also no objection to the exportation to Japan of the available maize.

The increase of the exportation of mineral oil and oil-products to Japan remains a matter of negotiation between the Japanese importers and the oil-producing companies. The present situation of oil-reserves does not, in the opinion of the Netherland Government, allow an increase of production. The same applies to the export of pitch cokes.

In the case of molasses, of which commodity, according to the figures in table III, the Japanese Government plan to import more than thirty times the normal quantity from the Netherlands Indies, no definite opinion can as yet be given.

The same applies to sisal fibre, where the quantity applied for is nearly twenty-five times the normal amount.

The available data concerning the exploitation of molybdenum ore, chrome-iron ore, wolfram ore and mica (" high quality ") seem to contradict the probability of exports of any importance.

The delegations met once more, on the 10th of June, at the request of Mr. Yoshizawa. It became quite clear at this meeting that the Japanese wished to wind up their business. They asked only for a number of technical elucidations in order to complete the report to their Government. But two other things also transpired. The first was that Mr. Yoshizawa still intended to advise acceptance of the Netherland proposals to his Minister. But in the second place he intimated that the freedom of action, which the Netherland Government had to reserve for themselves with respect to export quota, would most probably constitute an insuperable obstacle. The delegations parted in a subdued though friendly mood.

All this time the temper of Japanese publicity rose. The howls and imprecations at the totally unsatisfactory and insolent character of the Netherland answer, which the more savage Japanese correspondents in Batavia had reported, gave the impression that there could be only one remedy : war. The public became disquieted ; one could never be sure when the war of nerves would pass into the real thing. The general excitement even made people fail to notice a significant fact : after the decision on the negotiations had come up for discussion in Japan before a joint session of the Cabinet with the Army and Navy chiefs, the storm in the Press abated. It had ceased to be Mr. Matsuoka's own particular game.

On the 16th of June the Governor-General, in his opening speech for the annual session of the Volksraad, gave a concise and masterly survey of the situation. Without revealing the scope of the Japanese demands he stressed the firm and reasonable attitude maintained on our side, restating the Government's economic policy and its war-time modifications along the lines of our memoranda to the Japanese delegation. The attentive listener could not but understand that little appreciation for this attitude was expected in the impending final answer from Tokyo.

The next morning, 17th June 1941, Mr. Yoshizawa asked for an audience of the Governor-General, which was appointed for five o'clock in the afternoon at the still uncamou-flaged white palace in Batavia. Mr. Ishizawa, Dr. Van Mook, and Mr. Van Hoogstraten attended. Next door, in the main office of the Government Press Service, newspaper men and women of many nationalities and races were gradu-ally gathering for the fateful hand-out. The day was the 279th since Mr. Kobayashi landed.

After the usual compliments Mr. Yoshizawa opened the discussion by pointing out that the Japanese Government had drawn up their last proposals in an extremely conciliatory spirit, so much so that they would run great risks of general disapprobation if the document were to be published. Never-theless the answer of the Netherland delegation had been wholly unsatisfactory and therefore could not provide a sufficient basis for an agreement. He was instructed to ask the Governor-General to reconsider that answer ; if that were impossible, his Government had decided to discontinue the negotiations and to recall their delegation. The Governor-General replied that he appreciated the conciliatory attitude of the Japanese Government, but that the Netherland Government were candidly convinced that an agreement could not be reached on the terms proposed. In all sincerity he could not see his way to suggest any alterations in the standpoint of his Government as formulated in the last Netherland memorandum. He added, however, that in his judgment the negotiations had not been altogether unpro-ductive, although no agreement had emanated. The re-spective positions had been very searchingly and patiently analysed, and even if the parties could not agree, they had at least been able to come to a better understanding of each other.

Mr. Yoshizawa proceeded to state that, although the negotiations had brought no agreement, the Japanese Govern-ment wanted to see the general trade and economic relations maintained as hitherto. The Governor-General concurred. The failure to agree was to be expected, as the Netherlands

Indies could not extend their already very liberal policy in the manner recommended by the Japanese proposals, but this failure need leave no unfriendly sentiments. The Netherland Government would be satisfied to continue mutual relations on the old footing.

Mr. Yoshizawa then produced the draft of a joint *communiqué*, which, with a few minor amendments, was agreed upon in the following text, to be published forthwith :

Joint Communiqué

Both the Netherlands and the Japanese Delegations greatly regret that the economic negotiation, which has been conducted between them, has unfortunately come to no satisfactory result. It is needless, however, to add that the discontinuation of the present negotiation will lead to no change in the normal relations between the Netherlands Indies and Japan.

The Governor-General paid a general tribute to Mr. Yoshizawa's unflagging efforts and tact, whereupon Mr. Yoshizawa said that, however much he might be disappointed in the outcome, he had nothing but praise for the manner in which the negotiations had been conducted. In his opinion the gap between the respective views was largely due to the international situation. He had one more question to ask : Would the Netherlands Indies Government undertake to fulfil the assurances given in the last Netherland memorandum ? If so, the Japanese Government were prepared to purchase the agricultural products, of which the exports were not limited, to the amounts given in Table III of their last statement. This was agreed upon subject to the general qualifications stipulated by the Netherland Government. The matter of the oil-concessions would be further dealt with by the interested parties and the appropriate authorities. There would be no publication of details on either side. In conclusion Mr. Yoshizawa then announced the intended departure of himself and most of his delegation on 27th June. The audience had lasted precisely one hour.

A wave of relief swept over the country; it was certainly not felt least by those immediately concerned with the negotiations. A few journalists might have to tear up lurid accounts of ultimata and declarations of war, prepared in advance, but in the Press a congratulatory spirit prevailed, though tempered by a reasonable scepticism. It certainly looked like peace with honour. The Japanese delegation took their leave; several farewell dinners and the inevitable ceremony at Tandjong Priok saw the last of them. But on 22nd June Hitler invaded Russia and the war continued spreading on its relentless course.

CHAPTER VI

THE LAST MONTHS OF CRUMBLING PEACE

THEORETICALLY it was still possible for Japan to drop her plans of aggression and conquest and to emerge from the Second World War as the most prosperous industrial empire in Asia. Any discerning student of Far Eastern politics, however, knew that she could no longer do so of her own free will. In none of her previous wars had she been committed as she had committed herself during four years of conflict and rape in China. She could not back out, as she would have to if she wanted to restore good relations with the countries around the Pacific. Moreover, the chances of even richer booty really looked too alluring. After the first uneasy flutter about Hitler's attack on Russia, of which he seems to have given no previous intimation to his dear friends in Tokyo, the outlook became still more promising. The Tripartite Pact did not require Japan to join, and as the German Panzer divisions smashed their way across the Russian plains the ever-dreaded menace from Eastern Siberia and Vladivostok receded. The British Empire had to concentrate its forces in Europe and the Middle East and was considered a doomed concern by the more enthusiastic Axis partisans. The only dangerous opposition might come from the United States, but the whole width of the Pacific could be placed between that danger and Japanese aspirations.

The course upon which those Japanese aspirations had embarked became very clear in a few weeks. If Mr. Ito had unsuccessfully tried to obtain a signed agreement concerning the oil concessions before he sailed, he had done so only for his personal gratification. If Mr. Ishizawa, who remained as Consul-General, hopefully approached Mr. Van Hoogstraten on the 21st of June to talk about great purchases of sugar, maize, and sisal, it was either a smokescreen or the result of an incurable optimism. For Japanese merchantmen kept disappearing from their usual trade routes; there were constant rumours of landing drills in various places and of preparations for a move into Southern Indo-China; and new regulations came into force designed to put an end to most Japanese exports.

On the 7th of July the Japanese Government instituted a number of drastic export restrictions, which particularly affected the export of textiles and other commodities needed in the Indies. Of course, if war broke out with the British Empire and the United States, cotton would be scarce for a while in the Co-prosperity Sphere; it was a valid motive for husbanding stocks. And as Tokyo could not possibly imagine that an Allied attack was imminent, it looked like the preparation for Japanese action of a military character.

As a consequence of those regulations a number of Netherland merchants in Japan, who had bought and paid for considerable stocks of export goods, were faced with serious losses; the inadequate compensation offered by the Japanese authorities consisted, moreover, in practically frozen yen. Apart from the growing apprehension of impending aggression, these circumstances in themselves were sufficient to warrant a certain attachment of Japanese assets; preparations for a partial freezing were completed by the 24th of July.

By that same time reports from Tokyo, Saigon, and Vichy had made it almost certain that Japanese forces were ready to move or moving into Southern Indo-China and that they would occupy the important bases of Camranh Bay and Saigon, as they did a few days afterwards. After that Japan could proceed no further, except in Thailand, without directly invading American, British, or Netherland territory. It was obviously impossible to ignore the meaning and the intentions of this latest advance, and notwithstanding the fatuous plea of defence against British, Chinese, or De Gaullist aggression the Japanese themselves did not think it likely that it would be disregarded. But it will be interesting, after the war, to find out whether they reckoned with the possibility of war at that time, or whether they felt sure that Allied co-operation was still too rudimentary for really concerted and forceful action.

On Saturday afternoon, 26th July, a Reuter telegram brought the first news that the Government of the United States had suspended monetary and economic intercourse with Japan. This fact, if anything, proves that all the Japanese assertions about encirclement and agreed threats against Japan were just so many bare lies. The Governments concerned still reacted separately, and in a very mild way, against the most ominous steps taken by the military leaders in Tokyo. The American and British embargoes would remain without effect unless the Netherlands Indies joined in, and yet there was no collective action. It required a hurriedly convened meeting on Sunday afternoon and hard work during the evening and the night to have the necessary measures ready for execution throughout the Indies on Monday morning, before the banks opened their doors. These measures included the suspension of the monetary agreement with Japan and of all monetary transactions with that country, the application of the Exports Licensing Law to all exports towards the Japanese Empire, Manchuria, (Occupied) China, and Indo-China, and the subjection of the banks to a system of permits affecting monetary or credit transactions with Japanese subjects. Their announcement was made in the Volksraad when the session opened at 9 a.m. The spokesman for the Government, in making this announcement, reviewed the whole sequence of events, and emphasized that it was neither the intention to embarrass Japanese residents more than was unavoidable, nor to seal the door against further discussion. In retrospect it sounds almost unbelievably companionable.

Mr. Ishizawa, of course, lodged a protest, but never before had a Japanese protest been so patently *pro forma*. He was reminded of the fact that he had been warned by the Netherland delegation as long ago as March. And from that 28th of July onward the contacts between the Netherlands Indies and Japan virtually ceased.

A few ships removed the few paid goods waiting for transportation in the harbour godowns. Those sailing for Japan were packed with passengers; in the remaining months the Japanese population of the Indies dwindled from a peak of 7,000 to a bare 2,000. The celebrated oil contracts lapsed by default after some 900,000 tons had been delivered under their terms. The once buzzing Japanese merchant houses became silent and empty; their managers and employees were probably training for their jobs as economic experts with the invasion armies. Even the consulate-general had quieted down; its main business now was the booking of passages and the storage of personal effects and of increasing amounts of local currency. Only a few incidents with Japanese trying to smuggle forbidden goods out of the country enlivened the dull duties of liquidation.

Only one channel of communication seemed still functioning: the conversations in Washington. Hardly anything transpired about them, but though they might delay the explosion for some time, they could not be expected to turn the tide. Their development has since been made known through a detailed publication by the United States Government;[1] it only confirms the supposition that the gulf never narrowed. Mr. Kurusu started on his curiously Japanese mission of supervision and deceit when the attacking forces must have been assembling.

The position of the Netherlands Indies had been carefully analysed by the Netherland and the Netherlands Indies Governments. It is generally known now that the co-ordination of defence in the Far East was, even at this advanced date, for

---

[1] *Peace and War : United States Foreign Policy*, 1931-1941 ; pp. 113 *sqq.*

the greater part still embryonic. It was everybody's failure, to a greater or lesser degree, to perceive the inevitable consequences of Japanese aggression, but it seemed nobody's fault in particular ; the democracies simply could not adapt the old rules to the new game. The danger of defeat in the first round loomed large, but the requirements of the war in Europe loomed still larger. Reinforcements, if available, would have to be moved across enormous distances. But for a sudden and complete change of fortunes on the European and African battlefields—which did not occur—the attack would come and come suddenly ; since her trade with the world had disappeared, every succeeding month weakened Japan's position by a depletion of vital stocks. But how and wherever the attack might materialize, in one particular spot or at many places simultaneously, the course of action for the Indies was clear. Apart from the obligations of alliance with the British in the war with Germany, there was no sense in waiting until the attack specifically reached Netherlands Indies' territory. The Indies were probably the main Japanese objective ; if they did not want to succumb miserably and disgracefully, they would have to fight anyhow. In the coming fight all the meagre military resources in the Far East had to be pooled from the first day if the advance of the enemy was to be held long enough to prevent him from joining forces with his Axis partners, and to hold and consolidate bases from where a counter-attack might still be launched in due time. Both aims were achieved, be it at the last ramparts, and time was gained to wreck the most valuable conquests of the enemy before he reached them.

While the Indies were waiting for the attack they could but try to increase their armaments and their output of essential supplies. In the first matter they were dependent on others ; in the second they did their utmost. In 1939 they exported 378,000 tons of rubber ; in 1940 this was increased to 545,000 tons ; in 1941 the all-time record production of 1940 was again stepped up to 645,000 tons. An ever-increasing percentage went to the United States to enable them to expand war production and to build up stocks. The same applied to tin, where production rose from 31,500 tons in 1939 to 44,500 tons in 1940 and 52,500 tons in 1941. The production of high octane aviation spirit was started in April 1940 and rapidly expanded. The effort was maintained right to the end when, notwithstanding fearful losses, the inter-island ships kept snatching valuable cargoes from under the very spearheads of the Japanese invasion.

During the last days of November the imminence of a Japanese attack could no longer be doubted. The Netherland Fleet was ordered to sea, the Air Arm fully mobilized, officials on business in places north of the Indies were recalled. Information about enemy movements in the Gulf of Siam kept coming in ; even a direct attack on the Indies might be expected. At last, on the 8th of December,[1] just after 4 o'clock in the morning, the news came of the attack on Pearl Harbour ; within two hours reports followed of the bombing of Manila and Singapore. Between 6 and 7 a.m. the merchantmen were warned to make for the nearest safe port. And at 7 o'clock the clear, restrained voice of the Governor-General spoke over the radio : " Citizens of the Netherlands Indies ! In its unexpected attack on American and British territories, while diplomatic negotiations were still in progress, the Japanese Empire has consciously adopted a course of aggression. These attacks, which have thrown the United States and the British Empire into active war on the side of already fighting China, have as their objective the establishment of Japanese supremacy in the whole of East and South-East Asia. The aggression also gravely threatens the Netherlands Indies. The Netherland Government accepts the challenge and takes up arms against the Japanese Empire." [2]

[1] In the United States it should be remembered that the Indies lie West and Hawaii lies East of the date line : it was 7th December in Honolulu.

[2] On the same day, about 2.30 a.m., the Netherland Government in London cabled instructions to their Minister in Tokyo ; the telegram arrived on the

9th at night and on the 10th General Pabst handed the following letter to the Japanese Minister of Foreign Affairs (the original text was in French):

Mr. Minister,

By order of the Royal Government I have the honour to inform Your Excellency that, as Japan has opened hostilities against two powers with whom the Netherlands maintain particularly close relations, the Netherlands consider that a state of war exists between them and Japan.

The Swedish Government have agreed to take charge of the Netherland interests in Japan.

I beg Your Excellency to accept the assurance of my highest consideration.

(Signed)   J. C. PABST.

CHAPTER VII

RETROSPECT

As we look back across the valley of shadows where the Netherlands Indies lie hidden under Japanese occupation, we may ask whether the course of action, described in the preceding chapters, was the right one under the prevailing circumstances. A short review of the general situation can provide a tentative answer to that question.

The Netherlanders, the Indonesians, and the Indo-Chinese are essentially peaceful and inoffensive people. Not that they lack courage or, given proper training, military skill; in numerous cases during this war they have proved otherwise. But if again, as in Bacon's time, " the principal point of greatness in any State is to have a race of military men," this element of greatness had not been foremost in their thoughts and policies. The necessity of armament on a much larger scale than was required by a scrupulous neutrality, was only gradually appreciated by a nation that had no quarrel and could think of no quarrel with any one ; that had never joined the system of economic blocks into which the world was being parcelled out, and therefore had avoided being drawn into disputes about access to raw materials. It is a matter of common knowledge that many others, with less reason perhaps, have long shared this unsuspicious attitude.

In the Far East there might be reasons to mistrust Japanese expansionism, but it was still a far cry to outright southward aggression. It is true that Versailles and the Washington treaties of 1922, while curbing some of her more extreme ambitions, had increased the relative military strength of Japan. The Mandated Islands provided her with an advanced barrier to the South and East, whereas the agreed limitation of naval armaments and outpost fortifications worked out to the advantage of the most concentrated position and the least scrupulous party, i.e. in both respects to that of Japan. But there seemed to be so many obstacles in her path to southern conquest that the chances of a move in that direction appeared remote ; still more so when she entangled herself on the Asiatic mainland in the Manchurian affair.

It really was Hitler who opened wider prospects to the militarists in Tokyo. If Kaiser Wilhelm II had circulated postcards with his vision of a " yellow peril," Hitler's Government saw Far Eastern politics as a means to weaken their political opponents in Europe and to create future possibilities in Asia for the Herrenvolk. The Japanese were recognized as Aryans at an early date ; at the same time China was not neglected. In this game, however, Germany was probably more played with than playing ; her hands were too full on the other side of the world to get a real grip on Asiatic affairs. For the Japanese the prospect of a Second World War, in which their potential opponents in Asia would be engaged by the rapidly growing Nazi power, offered an opportunity to take sides a second time. Their last choice had been unexceptionable but rather barren of tangible results. Although Japan already possessed a considerable empire, she acted and felt like a have-not ; a feeling which was deepened by a world-wide opposition against her intrusive export policy. The indications were that, this time, she would make common cause with the aggressors.

When this danger became more clearly discernible, the Netherlands and the Netherlands Indies found a number of serious obstacles on the road to rearmament. They both lacked the basic minerals for a heavy industry : good iron ore and sufficient coking coal. The Indies had developed primarily as an agricultural country ; economic circumstances made it impossible for them to practise an autarchy that would have rendered them more independent from the purchase of weapons abroad. As yet there was no system of common defence against the increasing danger of aggression ;

8

those who criticized our prolonged neutrality simply tax us with not joining an organization that had ceased to exist since the League of Nations failed as an instrument against international banditry.   When the threatening clouds of war gathered, the limited markets for armaments became still more restricted ;   when Hitler precipitated the conflict by invading Poland, they almost closed down.

This was the more serious, because the system of defence decided upon in 1937-1938 was mainly based on a combination of naval and air power.   History has proved that it was the right decision, but the two arms on which it concentrated happened to be those with the highest ratio of modern equipment to the fighting man.   Incidentally it meant a very heavy expenditure, but contrary to what has been implied in some comments on the war in the East, no objections were raised on this point, notwithstanding the fact that both the Netherlands and the Netherlands Indies had been very hard hit by the economic crisis of 1930.   The course of world events prevented the execution of a programme that included three battle cruisers and a first line airplane strength of several hundred fighters and bombers ;   like all democracies we were outpaced in the first round by the rapidity of Axis preparations.

In some quarters comparisons have been made with China, and it has been suggested that we should have armed hundreds of thousands of Indonesians to wage war in the Chinese manner. Whoever is familiar with the Netherlands Indies must be convinced that such a course of action was impossible.   We had not been involved in an international war since Waterloo, with the exception of a short and localized campaign during the Belgian secession in 1830-1831.   In the Indies peace had reigned practically unbroken from the beginning of the twentieth century, and in the preceding seventy years local disturbances had been confined to comparatively few and remote corners of the Archipelago.   Since 1830 there had been no action in the Indies that could be compared, for instance, with the fighting in the Philippines after the Spanish-

American War. Consequently there was no soldiery like that in China, resulting from protracted internal and external conflicts ; to create one sufficiently well armed and organized would have taken many years. The growing Indonesian nationalism, which could, in time, provide the political foundation for a modern militia, was only slowly merging a dozen major groupings of the population into a unity that would eventually become strong enough to bear the strain of compulsory military service ; in the 'thirties this foundation was, as yet, too weak and too brittle. And even if this had not been the case, the necessary equipment in arms and ammunition could not be obtained at short notice.

Moreover, the nature of the country is not at all suited for the kind of fighting that has been going on in China for over six years. The main islands, with the exception of sparsely inhabited Borneo and New Guinea, are not more than 50 to 300 miles across. Their well-populated parts are easily accessible by a network of excellent roads. In the main island, Java, the jungle has almost disappeared ; where it still stands, in other islands, only small guerrilla parties can maintain themselves in its hardly penetrable and foodless recesses. There is either no room or no sustenance for manœuvre and flexible defence with large forces. An extensively but feebly armed population, unused to war, would have given the Japanese veteran divisions little trouble and would merely have been sacrificed in unavailing slaughter and misery. On the other hand, the invader might be expected to be most vulnerable while he was transporting his armies across the seas. If the attack could be beaten off it had to be done by naval and air power ; if only a delaying action remained possible, it was more effective to slow up sea transport than to wait until mechanized units had been landed.

It is idle to speculate upon the question, whether a well-prepared and full co-ordination of all the available American, British, Dutch, and Anzac forces in the Far East might have prolonged the initial struggle, or even fought the Japanese to a stand-still at a more advanced line of defence. For one thing, such a move on our side might have accelerated the Japanese attack, or changed its plan. As it was, neither the political nor the strategic thinking of the Allies and the Allies-to-be had yet reached that conception of combined operations and global warfare, in which the present phase of the struggle is being conducted. An experiment in unified command was initiated in January 1942, only to prove that such a command over heterogeneous forces in a wide and scattered theatre of war cannot be improvised, and needs months of careful preparation. Proposals for better co-ordination were made at various stages before the Japanese onslaught, but they only led to a few sketchy and disconnected results. In consequence the opportunities for a mobile defence in depth, offered by an island world stretching over 2,000 miles from North to South, with the mainland base of Australia at its southern extremity, were mostly lost and the several Allied forces were isolated and defeated in detail. But a more comprehensive plan of defence would probably have meant deliberate withdrawal from some of the main defensive positions, provided for in the various national and local schemes, which again might have been politically disastrous.

Under these circumstances the course of action of the Netherland and the Netherlands Indies Government had to be decided by their view on the imminence of a Japanese attack. As long as there was a chance of continued, if pre-carious, peace, they carefully avoided a provocative attitude, whilst firmly denying possible aid to the enemy and preventing any Japanese ascendancy over our affairs. When, however, the occupation of Southern Indo-China brought certainty with regard to Japanese intentions, only one way remained open. A contemptible hesitation to throw in our lot with those who stood on the same side, or an equally contemptible attempt at appeasement in the face of a direct threat, would have weakened the Allied position and strengthened the adversary. The war as a whole would go on ; victory could only be gained—and peace won—if all stood together. This war was indivisible ; we would have betrayed the common cause, had we tried to be belligerent in Europe and neutral in the Far East. The possibility was never even suggested.

Once the uncertainty about Japan's intentions had gone, it seemed to be the best tactics, as there could not be a full co-ordination of plans, to aim at least at as much co-ordination in action as could be achieved by individual decisions. The common front should appear as strong and determined as possible ; the common enemy, once Japan had declared herself as such, should derive as little profit as possible from lack of promptitude in the necessary counter-moves. In the actual fighting the same policy was applied, and historical analysis will probably prove that, whenever the Allied forces acted in combination against the Japanese expeditions while they were sea borne, they caused the greatest damage and delay ; whereas isolated actions on land, however courageous or even temporarily successful, failed to check the course of an enemy, who immeasurably exceeded us in army strength, and who could always by-pass an adversary brought to bay.

When defeat became inevitable, what remained to be done was the destruction of everything that could be of material assistance to the enemy, and the provision of safeguards for the non-combatant population in case of enemy occupation. The first was done—and generally speaking, done well—by the demolition of oil-wells, refineries, and mining equipment, the blocking and wrecking of harbours, dockyards, and workshops, the destruction of tools and stocks of war materials, and—when the last battles had been fought—the evacuation of everything that could still sail or fly, and of most of the naval and air personnel. For the second purpose food stocks were distributed and civil servants ordered to stay at their posts to aid and protect the people committed to their care. Wholesale destruction, even if it had been possible in so fertile a country, would not have deprived the Japanese of the necessary food and labour for their Army and their military requirements ; it would have been mere wanton cruelty towards the inhabitants, which the invader could not fail to exploit in the most damaging propaganda against ourselves and the United Nations.

Where mighty nations, for more than three years, were forced on the defensive by the concerted assaults of the Axis and failed to stem the onrush of the Japanese before it reached the limits of their plans of campaign, the invasion and the temporary occupation of the Netherlands Indies seemed a foregone conclusion. The mistakes that were made in the days of surprise attack and continuous retreat, when none of the Allies could escape the consequences of insufficient preparation, were of little importance as long as the main objectives of their defensive strategy—a maximum of enemy ships sunk at sea and of effective demolition ashore—were attained. How much the countries concerned were to suffer depended on their distance from the focus of aggression and the accessibility of their territory. The surrender of Indo-China and Thailand had offered an enormous advantage to the enemy ; but those of our Allies who had the time and the opportunity to recuperate, were assisted on their way to ultimate victory by the determined resistance in the Philippines Malaya, the Netherlands Indies, and Burma.

This, then, is the only just measure of the part played by the Netherlands Indies in the war : whether they did what was in their power to harm the enemy and to advance the cause of the Allies. It would appear that, by and large, such was the case in the period under review in this book. Acting on their own responsibility and in the face of overwhelming odds the Netherland Government and the Netherlands Indies did all they could to retard the Japanese attack and to restrict supplies to a potential enemy ; and when the cards were on the table they played their hand with decision, although it was almost wholly devoid of trumps.

OVERLEAF

particulars of publications

of similar interest

issued by

GEORGE ALLEN & UNWIN LTD

LONDON: 40 MUSEUM STREET, W.C. 1
CAPE TOWN: 73 ST. GEORGE'S STREET
TORONTO: 91 WELLINGTON STREET WEST
BOMBAY: 15 GRAHAM ROAD, BALLARD ESTATE
WELLINGTON, N.Z.: 8 KINGS CRESCENT, LOWER HUTT
SYDNEY, N.S.W.: AUSTRALIA HOUSE, WYNYARD SQUARE

Total War and the Human Mind

A PSYCHOLOGIST'S EXPERIENCES IN OCCUPIED HOLLAND

by Major A. M. Meerloo, M.D., F.R.S.M.

Crown 8vo   *5s. net*

This book by a Dutch psychologist and medical doctor, the author of several works on social psychology, has for its subject the effects of total war on the minds of men. Major Meerloo, having spent two years in Occupied Holland, was able to draw on his own experiences in discussing such themes as Mass Reaction to German Occupation, Hitler's Psychological Weapons, and the Psychology of Courage. The author gives an interesting account of the immediate effects of occupation, and the subsequent terror and disorganisation of daily life. He then proceeds to analyse those elements in the human character which make on the one hand for mass delusion of the German type, and on the other for mass and individual resistance as exemplified in Holland to-day. Major Meerloo stresses the importance of a psychological study of matters which are too often regarded as purely political. We must, he insists, realise that Democracy and Fascism are within us. He does not shrink from exposing the tendency of total war to bring to the fore the primitive and the adolescent elements in men, but he maintains that if men can only be brought to understand the springs of their actions, their innate desire for order will save them from ultimate destruction.

Military Operations in the Netherlands

FROM 10TH TO 17TH MAY, 1940

by P. L. G. Doorman

Crown 8vo   *With maps and plates*   *5s.*

This is the first detailed account of the invasion of Holland and the subsequent brief campaign, which was brought to an end by the tragic bombing of Rotterdam. Lt.-Colonel Doorman, who is a Staff Officer in the Dutch Army, has had access to all the material available at the present time, and his history is as complete as circumstances permit. He gives full particulars of the numbers and equipment of the Dutch forces engaged, and shows the various strategic and political considerations which determined their disposition on the eve of the attack.

This is a book for the specialist and the historian, but the general reader, too, will find much to interest him in this account, the military austerity of which serves to emphasise the heroic nature of its subject.

LONDON: GEORGE ALLEN & UNWIN LTD